```
641.566    Burnett, Mary Joyce.
B              Easy entertaining : holiday menus, recipes,
           and shopping lists / by Mary Joyce Burnett &
           Norma Sue Davis. -- Clifton, N.J. : Kingston
           Press, c1990.

              190 p. : ill.

              ISBN 0-940670-34-8: $19.95


                         cookery.    I. Davis, Norma Sue.
                        III. Title: Holiday menus,
                        and shopping lists.

                                                  89-80846
                                                      MARC
```

EASY ENTERTAINING: HOLIDAY MENUS, RECIPES, AND SHOPPING LISTS

*by MARY JOYCE BURNETT &
NORMA SUE DAVIS*

The Kingston Press, Inc.
Clifton, N.J. 07015

Copyright © 1990 The Kingston Press Inc.

All rights reserved.

No part of this publication may be reproduced, stored in a retrieval system, or transmitted, in any form, by any means, electronic, mechanical, photocopying, recording, or otherwise, without the prior permission of the publisher.

ISBN 0-940670-34-8

Illustrations by Mary-Dawn Burnett

Photo of Authors by Paul R. Cuppett

LC 89-80846

Published by

The Kingston Press, Inc.
P.O. Box 2759
Clifton, N.J. 07015

Printed in the United States of America

ACKNOWLEDGEMENT

When you achieve a worthwhile project, you never do it without the help of other people. We are indebted to many people who have helped and encouraged us in the writing of this book.

Mary Joyce thanks her loving Mother, Mary E. Goodman, who was a wonderful mentor and cook; her friend, Naomi Garner, a patient person who taught her the importance of planning menus; her immediate family, Don, Mary-Dawn and Doug, her biggest fans who are always willing to try her latest recipe; and her Texas Wesleyan University colleague, Margaret Patoski, who suggested she write a cookbook. Illustrations are by Mary-Dawn Burnett.

Norma Sue thanks Ursula and Bill Taylor, the best parents whose patience never failed and who taught her the art of entertainng at home; Dick Davis, her husband, who makes a house a home and is an unfailing supporter and confidant; her children and their spouses, Julia Denese and Terry McCants, Cheryl Sue (Suzie) and Harold Thomas, Amy Dawn and Paul Cuppett, and Dick Taylor and Sally Ann Davis; her grandchildren, Justin Lyn, Whitney Denese, and Austin Davis McCants, Jade Lauren, Lincoln Janai, Macy Laine, and London McCall Thomas, Calley Dawn and Hannah Kate Cuppett, who help by enjoying her cooking; and Bea and Jeff Davis who shared their wonderful cooking abilities.

And last but not least we are indebted to dear relatives and friends who have shared their recipes and entertained us in their homes.

INTRODUCTION

Cooking for family and friends is one of the joys of our lives. We enjoy entertaining at home. Thus our combined 70 years' experience "in the kitchen" will hopefully help you to achieve the same satisfaction we receive from the accolades of those who dine at our tables.

Since planning meals that are delicious, attractive, and healthful is not an easy task, we decided to share with you some of our favorite menus and recipes. The food you prepare will be not only delicious but also attractive to serve. To help you with your shopping, we have included a shopping list. You can do your shopping quickly if you will delete the items you have in your pantry from the list before doing your grocery shopping.

The Potpourri section includes helpful information we have collected over the years. The Microwave Shortcuts will help you spend your time wisely. Use the information in Helpful Hints, Gift Ideas, and Cooking a Turkey as the need arises.

TABLE OF CONTENTS

New Year's Eve Party 1
New Year's Day Buffet 12

Valentine Sweetheart Dinner 19
St. Patrick's Day Dinner 26

Family Easter Dinner 31
Mother's Day Brunch 38
Memorial Day Lunch 43

Father's Day Barbecue 48
Fourth of July Fiesta 55
Labor Day Buffet 63

Halloween Evening Dessert Buffet 69

Family Thanksgiving 79

Caroling Party 88
Christmas Eve Open House 95
Christmas Day Brunch 104
Christmas Dinner 112
Let's Get Rid of the Turkey Dinner 121

Substitute Recipes 125
Potpourri 168

NEW YEAR'S EVE PARTY

Serves 12

Hot Spice Punch

Banana Punch

Tasty Vegetable Dip

Lipton California Dip

Ham Dip

Chex Party Mix

Arkansas Hot Pepper Pecans

Fruit with Poppy Seed Dressing

Brunch Egg Casserole

Sweet Roll Biscuits

Crunchy Candy

Peanut Brittle

Pound Candy

Almond Cinnamon Cookies

Pina Colada Cake

Chocolate Sheet Cake

Shopping List

- 3 46-ounce cans unsweetened pineapple juice
- 9 cups cranberry juice cocktail
- 2 12-ounce cans frozen orange juice
- 1 12-ounce can frozen lemonade
- 1 9-ounce carton prepared whipped topping
- 2 kiwi fruit
- 1 pint strawberries
- 1 pound seedless grapes
- 9 bananas
- 6 medium apples
- 3 large oranges
- 1 large pineapple
- raw vegetables for dipping
- 1 15 1/2-ounce can cream of coconut (Coco Lopez)
- 6 32-ounce bottles carbonated lemon-lime drink
- 4 teaspoons sherry
- 1 teaspoon lemon juice
- 2 3/4 tablespoons onion juice
- 2/3 cup vinegar
- 4 teaspoons prepared mustard
- 14 dashes tabasco sauce
- 2 tablespoons worcestershire sauce
- 4 teaspoons soy sauce
- 2 cups vegetable oil
- Pam spray
- 11 cups sugar
- 1/2 cup Crisco
- 1 box powdered sugar
- 3 cups brown sugar
- 2 cups flour
- 1/4 cup honey
- 1 cup white Karo syrup
- 3 envelopes Lipton soup mix
- few grains cayenne pepper
- 4 teaspoons whole cloves
- 2 teaspoons seasoned salt
- 4 1/4 teaspoons salt
- 1 teaspoon curry powder
- 3 1/4 teaspoon dry mustard
- 2/3 teaspoon paprika
- 2 teaspoons vanilla
- 8 tablespoons cocoa

Shopping List, continued

1/2 teaspoon nutmeg
4 cinnamon sticks
2 teaspoons cinnamon
3 tablespoons poppy seed
2 teaspoons soda
3/4 teaspoon coconut flavoring
6 cups sour cream
2 8-ounce cartons small curd cottage cheese
2 2/3 cups margarine
3 3/4 cups real butter
8 eggs
6 tablespoons milk
1/2 cup buttermilk
2 cups half and half
4 cups shredded cheddar cheese
3 cans canned biscuits
crackers and chips for dips
1 lb. Hershey bar without nuts
2 2-ounce cans deviled ham
1 cup + 1 tablespoon mayonnaise

1 Duncan Hines white cake mix
ingredients for the cake mix
1 box cinnamon graham crackers
1 large can chow mein noodles
4 cups corn Chex
4 cups rice Chex
4 cups wheat Chex
3 cups raw peanuts
1 1/2 cups salted nuts
1 large can mixed nuts
2 small packages sliced almonds
6 cups pecan halves
1 12-ounce package butterscotch bits
1 12-ounce package semisweet chocolate chips
1 7-ounce can coconut
6 slices white bread
1 pound ground sausage
waxed paper

HOT SPICE PUNCH

In the bottom of 30 cup percolator, put:

9 cups unsweetened pineapple juice
9 cups cranberry juice cocktail
4 1/2 cups water

In percolator basket, put:

1 cup brown sugar
4 teaspoons whole cloves
4 cinnamon sticks, broken
1/4 teaspoon salt

Allow to go through perk cycle. Serve piping hot. Keep any leftover punch in cocktail juice jars in refrigerator. Reheat and serve unexpected holiday guests.

Makes 30 cups

BANANA PUNCH

1 46-ounce can pineapple juice
2 12-ounce cans frozen orange juice
1 12-ounce can frozen lemonade
6 bananas

6 32-ounce bottles carbonated lemon-lime drink
4 cups sugar
6 cups water

Dissolve sugar in water. Add pineapple juice, orange juice and lemonade. Mash bananas and add to mixture. Add carbonated drink just before serving.

Makes 50 cups

NOTE: Mixture may be frozen. Before serving remove mixture from freezer to allow to thaw partially and add carbonated beverage just before serving.

TASTY VEGETABLE DIP

2 cups sour cream
1 cup + 1 tablespoon mayonnaise
1 teaspoon curry powder
1/4 teaspoon dry mustard
4 teaspoons sherry

4 teaspoons prepared mustard
1 teaspoon salt
2/3 teaspoon paprika
few grains cayenne pepper

Combine all ingredients at least one hour before serving and refrigerate. Serve with your favorite raw vegetables.

Serves 12

LIPTON CALIFORNIA DIP

1 envelope Lipton onion soup mix   1 pint dairy sour cream

Pour an envelope of Lipton onion soup mix into a pint of dairy sour cream. Stir with a fork. Chill. It's ready to serve with potato chips, celery, crackers—everything dippable.

Makes 1 1/4 cups

HAM DIP

2 8-ounce cartons small-curd cottage cheese
2 packages onion soup mix

2 2-ounce cans deviled ham
1 pint sour cream
dash tabasco sauce

Mix all ingredients well and serve with crackers or potato chips.

Serves 12

CHEX PARTY MIX

2/3 cup margarine
2 tablespoons worcestershire sauce
2 teaspoons seasoned salt

4 cups corn Chex
4 cups rice Chex
4 cups wheat Chex
1 1/2 cups salted nuts

Heat oven to 250 degrees. Melt butter in shallow pan over low heat. Stir in worcestershire sauce and seasoned salt. Add Chex and nuts. Mix over low heat until all pieces are coated. Heat in oven 45 minutes. Stir every 15 minutes. Spread on absorbent paper to cool.

Makes 14 cups

ARKANSAS HOT PEPPER PECANS

1/4 cup butter
2 cups pecan halves
4 teaspoons soy sauce

1 teaspoon salt
12 dashes Tabasco sauce

Melt butter in baking pan. Spread pecans evenly in pan and bake at 300 degrees for 30 minutes. Combine soy sauce, salt, and Tabasco sauce, and toss with pecans. Spread on paper towels to cool.

Serves 12

FRUIT WITH POPPY SEED DRESSING

1 1/2 cups sugar
2 teaspoons dry mustard
1 teaspoon salt
2/3 cup vinegar
2 3/4 tablespoons onion juice
2 cups vegetable oil, not olive oil
3 tablespoons poppy seeds
1 teaspoon lemon juice
1/4 cup honey
Assorted fresh fruit in bite-size pieces

Mix sugar, mustard, salt, vinegar, lemon juice, and onion juice and stir thoroughly. Slowly add oil, beating constantly after each addition and continuing to beat until thick. Add honey, poppy seeds and beat for two minutes. This dressing is easier to make in a blender or food processor, or with an electric mixer using medium speed. Refrigerate.
NOTE: This dressing may be kept in refrigerator for two weeks.

Makes 4 1/4 cups

BRUNCH EGG CASSEROLE

6 slices white bread, crust removed
1 pound ground sausage
4 cups shredded Cheddar cheese
6 eggs
1 teaspoon salt
1 teaspoon dry mustard
2 cups half and half

Lightly butter each slice of bread. Place bread in a 9x13" buttered glass baking dish. Brown sausage. Drain and pat with paper towels. Sprinkle sausage over bread. Sprinkle cheese over sausage. Beat eggs. Add salt, dry mustard, and half and half. Beat again. Pour egg mixture over bread, sausage, and cheese.

At this point, the dish may be covered with foil and refrigerated overnight or frozen until ready to use. Remove from freezer and thaw overnight in refrigerator. Remove foil. Bake 45 minutes at 350 degrees or until casserole is bubbly and lightly browned on top. This dish reheats easily.

Serves 12

SWEET ROLL BISCUITS

3 cans canned biscuits
2 sticks butter
2 cups brown sugar
1 cup chopped nuts
1 teaspoon cinnamon
1/2 teaspoon nutmeg
Pam or other brand of shortening spray

Spray bundt pan with shortening. Divide each biscuit into four pieces. Place 1/2 of biscuits in pan. Melt butter and brown sugar in microwave; boil 1 minute. Add to butter and brown sugar, cinnamon, nutmeg, and nuts. Pour half of butter mixture on half of biscuits. Place other half of biscuits in pan and pour other half of butter mixture on top. Bake at 400 degrees for 20 minutes and continue baking at 350 degrees for 25 minutes. After removing from oven, leave biscuits in pan for 10 minutes, then invert on platter. *Serves 12*

CRUNCHY CANDY

1 12-ounce package butterscotch bits
1 12-ounce package semisweet chocolate chips
Large can chow mein noodles
Large can mixed nuts

Melt butterscotch bits and chocolate chips. Stir in noodles and mixed nuts. Drop tablespoon size pieces on waxed paper. Remove from paper when firm. *Serves 12*

PEANUT BRITTLE

1 cup sugar
1 cup white Karo syrup
1/2 cup water

3 cups raw peanuts
Dash of salt
1 heaping teaspoon soda

Cook together sugar, Karo, and water until clear, and sugar is dissolved. Add raw peanuts, cook and stir occasionally until mixture becomes golden in color. (You will smell the peanuts as they become roasted.) Add salt and soda, stirring quickly. Pour mixture on buttered cookie sheet, which should be set on cake rack. Cool. Break into pieces.

POUND CANDY

1 pound butter
2 cups white sugar

1 pound nuts
1 pound Hershey bar without nuts

Cook butter and sugar in heavy skillet rather fast, stirring constantly until the mass reaches the crack stage in cold water. Pour mixture over nuts in well-greased pan while still very hot. Immediately break into bits the Hershey bar and scatter over mixture. When cold, crack into pieces to remove from pan.

NOTE: Crack stage—syrup when dropped into very cold water separates into threads which are hard and brittle.

ALMOND CINNAMON COOKIES

1 box cinnamon graham crackers
1/2 cup real butter
1/2 cup margarine
1/2 cup sugar
2 small packages sliced almonds

Break crackers at perforations and place on foil-lined baking sheet with sides. Boil butter, margarine, and sugar for 2 minutes. Spoon over crackers and sprinkle with almonds. Bake for 7 to 8 minutes at 350 degrees. Remove cookies from foil when taken from the oven and allow to cool.

PINA COLADA CAKE

1 Duncan Hines White cake mix
1 7-ounce can coconut
1 15 1/2-ounce can cream of coconut (Coco Lopez)
1 9-ounce carton prepared whipped topping
3/4 teaspoon coconut flavoring

Prepare cake mix according to package directions adding one half of the canned coconut to the batter. Bake in a greased and floured 13x9x2" pan. When done, remove from oven and punch holes in cake with fork. Pour cream of coconut into holes. Let sit about 5 minutes or until warm. Ice with the following: Mix well thawed prepared topping, $3\frac{1}{2}$ ounces coconut, and coconut flavoring. Refrigerate. *Serves 12*

CHOCOLATE SHEET CAKE

2 cups sugar
2 cups flour
1 stick margarine
1/2 cup Crisco
4 tablespoons cocoa
1 cup water
1/2 cup buttermilk
2 eggs, slightly beaten
1 teaspoon cinnamon
1 teaspoon soda
1 teaspoon vanilla

Icing:
1 stick margarine
4 tablespoons cocoa
6 tablespoons milk
1 box powdered sugar
1 teaspoon vanilla
1 cup pecans (optional)

Put sugar and flour in mixing bowl and mix well. In sauce pan, combine margarine, Crisco, cocoa, and water. Bring to a rapid boil. Then pour over first mixture. Beat well. Add buttermilk, 2 eggs (slightly beaten), cinnamon, soda, and vanilla. Pour into greased floured 9x13 or larger pan. Bake 20 minutes at 400 degrees.

Icing:
Bring margarine, cocoa, and milk to a rapid boil. Add powdered sugar, vanilla, and pecans (optional). Beat until smooth and pour over hot cake.

NEW YEAR'S DAY BUFFET

Serves 10

Fruit Punch

Knorr's Spinach Dip with French Bread

Garden Salad with Oranges and Almonds

Yummy Baked Chicken with Rice

Good Luck Blackeyed Peas

Perfect Chocolate Cake with

Chocolate Cream Filling and Chocolate Buttercreme Frosting

Coffee Ole

Shopping List

1 12-ounce can frozen orange juice
1 6-ounce can frozen lemon juice
1 46-ounce can pineapple juice
1 large can apricot nectar
3/4 small bottle almond extract
1/4 cup vinegar
1 cup real mayonnaise
1 cup vegetable oil
2 1/4 cups flour
1 teaspoon baking soda
2 teaspoons salt
black pepper (dash)
red pepper (dash)
1 tablespoon parsley flakes
3/4 teaspoon cinnamon
10 sticks cinnamon
nutmeg (dash)
4 1-ounce squares unsweetened chocolate
1 tablespoon baking cocoa
3 cups sugar
3 1/2 teaspoons vanilla
2 3/4 cups powdered sugar
6 ounces semisweet chocolate pieces
1 20-ounce package frozen chopped spinach
1 22-ounce can mandarin oranges
6 tablespoons chocolate syrup
6 cups brewed coffee
2 cans cream of chicken or cream of mushroom soup
1 package Knorr's vegetable soup mix
1 can water chestnuts
2 jars chipped beef
rice for 10 servings
1 pound dried blackeyed peas
1 cup sliced or slivered almonds
4 cups whipping cream
1 cup buttermilk
1 cup margarine
1 cup butter
28 ounces sour cream
4 eggs
10 chicken breasts, boned
10 bacon strips

Shopping List, continued

1/2 pound salt pork
1 head iceberg lettuce
1 head romaine lettuce
5 cloves of garlic

9 green onions
1 large onion
1 loaf French bread

FRUIT PUNCH

1 12-ounce can frozen orange juice
1 6-ounce can frozen lemon juice
1 46-ounce can pineapple juice
1 large can apricot nectar
1/2 cup sugar
3/4 small bottle almond extract

Dilute frozen juice as directed. Mix all ingredients and chill.

Makes 17 cups

KNORR'S SPINACH DIP

1 20-ounce package frozen chopped spinach
1 package Knorr vegetable soup mix
1 1/2 cups sour cream
1 cup real mayonnaise
3 chopped green onions
1 can sliced water chestnuts

Thaw spinach and squeeze water from it. Combine ingredients and mix well. Let chill overnight to expand dried veggies. Use bite-size pieces of French bread to dip with. NOTE: Hollow out French bread loaf to use as a container for the dip.

Serves 10

GARDEN SALAD WITH ALMONDS AND ORANGES

1 head iceberg lettuce
1 head romain lettuce
1 cup sliced or slivered almonds
1/4 cup sugar
6 green onion tops, thinly sliced
1 22-ounce can mandarin oranges, chilled and drained

Dressing:
1 cup vegetable oil
1/4 cup vinegar
1/4 cup sugar
1 teaspoon salt
Dash black pepper
Dash red pepper
1 tablespoon parsley flakes

Wash and prepare lettuce. Tear into bite-size pieces. Chill. Combine almonds and sugar in a saucepan. Stir over medium heat until sugar melts and is browned. Cool caramelized almonds on a cookie sheet, and break into tiny pieces. Combine all ingredients for dressing and chill. When ready to serve, combine lettuce, green onions, almonds and oranges. Toss with desired amount of dressing.

Serves 10

YUMMY BAKED CHICKEN WITH RICE

10 chicken breasts, boned and skinned
2 jars chipped beef
2 10.5-ounce cans cream of chicken *or* cream of mushroom soup
2 8-ounce cartons sour cream
10 raw bacon strips
rice for 10 servings

Salt and pepper each chicken piece; wrap one bacon strip around each. Mix together soup and sour cream. Tear chipped beef into small pieces. Layer chicken, beef, and soup-cream mixture in deep baking dish. Bake at 250 degrees for 3 hours. Spoon gravy over chicken to serve over rice.

Serves 10

GOOD LUCK BLACKEYED PEAS

1 pound dried blackeyed peas
1/2 pound salt pork
1 large onion, chopped
red pepper to taste
3 cloves garlic
salt to taste

Wash peas and cover with water; soak overnight. Add salt pork, peas, onion, red pepper, and garlic. Cook slowly about two hours. Season peas with salt.

Serves 10

THE PERFECT CHOCOLATE CAKE

3 1-ounce squares unsweetened chocolate
1/2 cup water
2 1/4 cups all-purpose flour
1 teaspoon baking soda
1 cup (2 sticks) butter, softened
1 1/2 cups sugar (divided for use)
4 eggs, separated (divided for use)
1 teaspoon vanilla
1 cup buttermilk

Preheat oven to 350 degrees. Grease and flour 3 9-inch round cake pans. Combine chocolate and water in small sauce pan and set over very low heat. Cook, stirring vigorously, until chocolate melts and mixture is smooth. Remove from heat and set aside to cool. Combine flour, baking soda, and salt; sift together onto a large piece of wax paper. Put the butter and 1 cup sugar into a large mixing bowl and beat until smooth and well blended. Add egg yolks 1 at a time, beating well after each addition. Add vanilla and cooled chocolate mixture; beat until blended. Add sifted dry ingredients in 3 parts alternately with buttermilk, beating after each addition, until the batter is smooth. In a separate mixing bowl, beat egg whites and remaining 1/2 cup sugar until whites are stiff but moist. Gently stir 1/3 of the whites into the batter. Add remaining whites and fold them in. Divide batter among pans. Bake 25-30 minutes. Let cool in pan 5 minutes before turning onto racks. Spread with Chocolate Cream Filling and Buttercreme Frosting.

Serves 10

CHOCOLATE CREAM FILLING

1 cup well-chilled whipping cream
1/4 cup confectioners sugar
1 tablespoon baking cocoa
1 teaspoon vanilla extract

In medium bowl, beat with electric mixer whipping cream, confectioners sugar, unsweeetened baking cocoa, and vanilla extract. Refrigerate until ready to use.

CHOCOLATE BUTTERCREME FROSTING

6 ounces semisweet chocolate pieces
1/2 cup half and half cream
1 cup (2 sticks) butter or margarine
2 1/2 cups confectioners sugar

In medium saucepan, combine chocolate pieces, half and half, and butter, stirring over medium heat until smooth. Remove from heat and stir in confectioners sugar. Set bowl over a second larger bowl filled with ice. Beat with electric mixer until it holds shape. Frost cake.

COFFEE OLE

6 tablespoons chocolate syrup
1 1/2 cup heavy cream
3/4 teaspoon ground cinnamon
6 tablespoons sugar
1 1/2 teaspoons vanilla
pinch of nutmeg
6 cups strong, hot coffee
whipped cream for topping

Place the chocolate syrup, heavy cream, cinnamon, sugar, vanilla, and nutmeg into a small bowl. Stir and then whip until well blended. Pour hot coffee into 10 mugs and add the chocolate syrup mixture, stirring gently. Top with whipped cream and sprinkle with extra cinnamon. Use cinnamon sticks for stirrers if desired.

Serves 10

VALENTINE SWEETHEART DINNER

Serves 6

Clear Tomato Soup

Cheese Strips

Sunburst Fruit Salad

Marinated Beans

Horseradish Roast

Company Potatoes

Buttered Carrots and Celery

Strawberry Cake

Shopping List

- 4 pound arm roast
- 2 pints sour cream
- 2 cups butter
- 1 cup margarine
- 1 8-ounce package cream cheese
- 1 cup grated sharp cheese
- 1/2 cup Parmesan cheese
- 1 5-ounce bottle horseradish
- 2 10-ounce boxes frozen strawberries
- 1 can whole green beans
- 1 can whole yellow beans
- 1 can French style green beans
- 1 can red kidney beans
- 1 small can chopped pimento
- 1 20-ounce can pineapple tidbits
- 2 cans mandarin oranges
- 4 cups canned tomato juice
- 2 cups chicken consomme
- 1 white cake mix
- 1 7-ounce can coconut
- 1 8-ounce package miniature marshmallows
- 1 can Eagle Brand condensed milk
- 1 teaspoon red food coloring
- 1 teaspoon green food coloring
- 1/4 teaspoon vanilla
- 1 6-ounce package strawberry jello
- 1/2 cup chopped nuts
- 1 small package slivered almonds
- 2 1/2 cups flour
- 3 1/2 teaspoons salt
- 1 cup sugar
- 1 bottle red sugar
- 1 bottle green sugar
- 1 box powdered sugar
- 1 teaspoon garlic salt
- 1/2 teaspoon white pepper
- 1 1/2 teaspoons black pepper
- 1/8 teaspoon cayenne pepper
- 6 whole cloves garlic
- 2 teaspoons paprika
- 1 bay leaf
- 1/8 teaspoon thyme
- 3/4 cup vinegar

Shopping List, continued

1 cup Wesson oil
1 green pepper
5 cups celery
2 large onions

6 medium carrots
2 sprigs parsley
8 medium Irish potatoes
1/2 cup red wine

CLEAR TOMATO SOUP

1/4 cup diced celery
1/4 cup diced carrots
1/4 cup diced onion
2 tablespoons butter
2 sprigs parsley
4 cups canned tomato juice
1/2 teaspoon white pepper
6 cloves garlic
1 bay leaf
1 teaspoon salt
1/8 teaspoon thyme
2 cups canned chicken consomme

Saute celery, carrots, and onion in the butter for 5 minutes. Add rest of ingredients except consomme and bring to a boil. Cover and simmer over heat for one hour. Strain, add consomme, heat and serve.

Serves 6

CHEESE STRIPS

1 cup butter
1 cup finely grated sharp cheese
2 cups flour
1 teaspoon salt
1/8 teaspoon cayenne pepper
1/2 cup Parmesan cheese

Mix all ingredients (butter and cheese at room temperature) and roll out very thin, cutting into narrow strips. Sprinkle lightly with Parmesan cheese. Bake at 350 degrees for 15 minutes.

Makes 5 dozen

SUNBURST FRUIT SALAD

2 cans mandarin oranges, drained
1 20-ounce can pineapple tidbits, drained
1 3 to 4-ounce can coconut
1 8-ounce package miniature marshmallows
1 pint sour cream

Mix ingredients together and refrigerate for two hours.

Serves 6

MARINATED BEANS

1 can whole green beans
1 can whole yellow beans
1 can French style green beans
1 can red kidney beans
1 small can chopped pimento
1 medium onion, chopped
1/2 green pepper, chopped

Drain and rinse beans; add other ingredients. Marinate for 24 hours in the following dressing:
 3/4 cup sugar
 3/4 cup vinegar
 1/3 cup salad oil
Mix until sugar is dissolved and pour over beans. Drain to serve. Keeps for a week in refrigerator.

Serves 6

HORSERADISH ROAST

4 pound arm roast
1 5-ounce bottle horseradish
1 large sliced onion
Salt
Pepper
1/2 cup red wine

Brown roast unfloured. Add salt, pepper, sliced onions, horseradish, and red wine. Bake at 325 degrees for 4 to 5 hours in covered roasting pan.

Serves 6

COMPANY POTATOES

8 medium potatoes, cooked
1 8-ounce package cream cheese, at room temperature
1 12-ounce carton sour cream
1 teaspoon garlic salt
1/2 cup butter
1/2 teaspoon paprika

Cook and mash potatoes; add cream cheese, beating until smooth. Add sour cream, garlic salt, and lots of butter. Place in a 1 1/2- to 2-quart casserole. Dot with butter. Sprinkle with paprika. Bake uncovered in a 350 degree oven for 30 minutes or in a 250 degree oven for 1 hour.
NOTE: If desired, prepare the day before serving, refrigerate and bake the following day.

Serves 6

BUTTERED CARROTS AND CELERY

5 medium carrots, cut into strips
4 stalks celery, cut into strips
1/2 cup water
2 tablespoons butter, melted
1 1/2 teaspoon sugar
1/2 teaspoon salt
1/8 teaspoon pepper
2 tablespoons butter, melted

Combine first 7 ingredients in a 2-quart baking dish. Cover and bake at 350 degrees for 45 minutes. Drain. Add 2 tablespoons butter, tossing to coat.

Serves 6

STRAWBERRY CAKE

Cake:
1 white cake mix
2/3 cup Wesson oil
1 3-ounce package strawberry jello
1/2 cup water
4 tablespoons flour
1 10-ounce box frozen strawberries, thawed

Icing:
1/2 cup butter
1 box powdered sugar
1/2 10-ounce box frozen strawberries, thawed

Preheat oven to 350 degrees. Grease and flour sheath cake pan which is 12x17 inches in size. Mix all ingredients together and bake 12 to 14 minutes. Cool; ice.
NOTE: If you want to decorate cake, prepare Strawberry Candy (recipe follows).

STRAWBERRY CANDY

1 3-ounce package strawberry jello
6 tablespoons Eagle Brand condensed milk
1 teaspoon red food coloring
1/4 teaspoon vanilla
1/2 cup angel flake coconut

1/2 cup chopped nuts
dash salt
1/2 small package slivered almonds
Green food coloring
Red sugar
Green sugar

Mix together dry jello and Eagle Brand milk. Add red food coloring, vanilla, angel flake coconut, finely chopped nuts, and salt. Put in refrigerator for 1/2 hour or more. Scoop onto wax paper with teaspoon. Make into small balls about the size of a walnut. Put back into refrigerator for another 1/2 hour or longer. Shape into strawberries, roll in red sugar, dip end in green sugar, and insert green colored slivered almonds for stem. Keep covered in refrigerator.
NOTE: Color sliced almonds for stems by dipping in green food coloring. Allow stems to dry. You may prepare stems the day before.
Makes 25-30 sugared strawberries

ST. PATRICK'S DAY DINNER

Serves 6

St. Patrick's Punch
Cherry Jello Waldorf Salad
Stuffed Pork Chops
Green Vegetable Medley
Potato Casserole
Key Lime Pie

Shopping List

- 6 double-loin pork chops with pockets for stuffing
- 6 eggs
- 1 cup light cream
- 4 ounces sour cream
- 1/2 cup butter
- 1 10-ounce package frozen green beans
- 1 10-ounce package frozen lima beans
- 1 10-ounce package frozen peas
- 1/2 cup Parmesan cheese
- 8 ounces Cheddar cheese
- 4 ounces mayonnaise
- 1 can cream of chicken soup
- 3 cups bread crumbs
- 3/4 cup sugar
- 1/2 teaspoon cream of tartar
- 1 can sweetened condensed milk
- 1 3-ounce package lime jello
- 1 3-ounce package cherry jello
- 1 tablespoon salt
- 1 tablespoon pepper
- 2 teaspoons poultry seasoning
- 2 teaspoons almond extract
- green food coloring (few drops)
- 1/4 cup red hot cinnamon candies
- 1/2 cup pecans
- 1 1/2 cups bottled lime juice
- 1 12-ounce can frozen limeade concentrate
- 45 ounces Sprite
- 1/2 cup green pepper
- 6 medium Irish potatoes
- 4 medium apples
- 3 medium onions
- 2 stalks celery
- toothpicks

ST. PATRICK'S PUNCH

1 3-ounce package lime flavored gelatin
1 cup hot water
1/4 to 1 cup bottled lime juice
1 12-ounce can frozen limeade concentrate
45 ounces Sprite
2 teaspoons almond extract
green food coloring (several drops)

Dissolve gelatin in hot water. Then stir in frozen limeade concentrate; add lime juice. To serve, pour into bowl over 1 1/2 quarts cracked ice. Add Sprite.

Makes 24 4-ounce servings

CHERRY JELLO WALDORF SALAD

1 3-ounce package cherry jello
1 cup hot water
1/4 cup red hot cinnamon candies
1 cup celery, chopped
1 cup apples, chopped
1/2 cup pecans, chopped

Dissolve 1 package cherry jello in 1 cup hot water. Dissolve 1/4 cup of red hot cinnamon candies in 1/2 cup boiling water to melt red hots. Add red hots and another 1/4 cup water to jello. Cool. Add 1 cup celery, 1 cup apples and 1/2 cup pecans.

Serves 6

STUFFED PORK CHOPS

6 double-loin pork chops with pockets for stuffing
salt
black peppercorns
3 cups dry bread crumbs

1 1/4 cups onion, chopped
1 1/2 cups apple, chopped
2 teaspoons poultry seasoning
1 cup light cream, approximately
toothpicks

Have butcher cut pockets for stuffing in 6 double loin pork chops. Take a sharp knife and deepen and widen these pockets yourself, being careful not to cut through the top or bottom of the chop. Season inside and out with salt and freshly ground black pepper, and stuff to capacity with the following dressing:

Mix fine, dry bread crumbs, onion, apple (peeled, cored, and minced), salt, freshly ground pepper, and poultry seasoning. Add sufficient cream to moisten. Fasten the bulging chops with toothpicks and sear in a hot iron skillet until brown. Stand the chops on end first, so that the fat melts and greases the skillet. When they have browned on both sides, place the chops in an iron or earthenware casserole, piling any extra dressing on top. (It is a good idea to save a little dressing just for this purpose.) Cover and bake in a 350 degree oven for 1 1/2 hours, basting often.

Serves 6

GREEN VEGETABLE MEDLEY

1 10-ounce package frozen green beans
1 10-ounce package frozen lima beans
1 10-ounce package frozen peas
1/2 cup diced green bell pepper, optional

1/2 cup diced onion
1/8 cup butter
4 ounces sour cream
4 ounces mayonnaise
salt and pepper to taste
grated Parmesan cheese

Cook vegetables according to package directions. Drain. Saute bell pepper and onion in butter until tender. Mix all ingredients thoroughly. Top with Parmesan cheese. Serve immediately.

Serves 6

POTATO CASSEROLE

6 large potatoes, sliced and cooked in salt water for about 5 minutes
8 ounces cheddar cheese, grated
1 medium onion, grated
1/3 cup butter
1 can cream of chicken soup mixed with 1 can water
black pepper to taste

Layer potatoes, cheese, onion, butter, and pepper. Cover with soup mixture. Bake in 400 degree oven for 45 minutes.

Serves 6

KEY LIME PIE

4 egg yolks
6 egg whites
1 can sweetened condensed milk
1/2 cup lime juice
3/4 cup sugar
1/2 teaspoon cream of tartar

Beat egg yolks until lemon colored. Blend in condensed milk slowly. Add lime juice and mix well. In another bowl add cream of tartar to egg whites and beat until foamy. Continue beating, adding sugar one tablespoon at a time until egg whites peak. Fold 6 tablespoons of the meringue into the filling mixture. Pour into a 9" baked pie shell. Top with meringue and bake in a slow 325 degree oven until golden brown. NOTE: You may add 5 drops green food coloring to pie filling.

Serves 6

FAMILY EASTER DINNER

Serves 12

Pink Salad

Cauliflower Salad

Cranberry-Burgundy Glazed Ham

Sweet Potato Casserole

Green Bean Casserole

Honey-Cornmeal Biscuits

Banana Split Squares

Shopping List

1 head iceberg lettuce
1 head cauliflower
2 cloves garlic
1/2 purple onion
1 medium green bell pepper
1 cup sliced celery
2 chopped onions
7 bananas
1 10 to 14 pound bone-in fully cooked ham
1 pound bacon
1/2 cup sour cream
4 3/4 sticks margarine
1 stick butter
1/2 cup milk
2 eggs
1/2 cup honey
2 teaspoons prepared mustard
1 3/4 cups Bisquick baking mix

1/2 cup yellow cornmeal
1 3/8 cups brown sugar
2 cups powdered sugar
1/4 cup sugar
1/2 box whole cloves
1 teaspoon grated orange peel
dash salt
1/4 teaspoon cinnamon
1/4 teaspoon nutmeg
1 teaspoon vanilla
1 cup lemon juice
1/2 cup mayonnaise
1 can cherry pie filling
3/4 cup evaporated milk
1 can sweetened condensed milk
1 60-ounce can sweet potatoes
4 cans French style green beans
2 small cans sliced water chestnuts

Shopping List, continued

- 2 cans cream of chicken soup
- 2 20-ounce cans crushed pineapple
- 1 16-ounce can whole cranberry sauce
- 1 small jar maraschino cherries
- 2 large containers prepared whipped topping
- 1 cup grated Parmesan cheese
- 3 cups graham cracker crumbs
- 2 cups buttered bread crumbs
- 2 cups pecans
- 1 regular size bag marshmallows
- 1/2 cup burgundy wine

PINK SALAD

1 large can crushed pineapple, drained
1 can cherry pie filling
1 can sweetened condensed milk
1 large container prepared topping
1 cup chopped pecans

Mix together in large bowl and chill before serving.

Serves 12

CAULIFLOWER SALAD

1 head iceberg lettuce, torn into bite size pieces
1 head cauliflower, cut into very small florets
1/2 purple onion, thinly sliced
1 pound bacon, crisply cooked and crumbled
1 medium green bell pepper, chopped
1 cup thinly sliced celery
1 cup grated Parmesan cheese
1/8 to 1/4 cup sugar
1/2 cup mayonnaise
1/2 cup sour cream

In serving bowl, layer lettuce, cauliflower, onion, bacon, bell pepper, celery, and cheese. Repeat layers. Sprinkle sugar over all. Mix mayonnaise and sour cream together and spread on top. Seal and chill in refrigerator overnight. Toss well before serving.

Serves 12

CRANBERRY-BURGUNDY GLAZED HAM

1 bone-in fully cooked ham (about 10 to 14 pounds)
1/2 box whole cloves
1 pound can whole cranberry sauce
1 cup brown sugar
1/2 cup burgundy wine
2 teaspoons prepared mustard

Place ham, fat side up, in shallow roasting pan. Score fat in diamond pattern; stud with whole cloves. Insert meat thermometer. Bake in slow oven (325 degrees) for 2 1/2 to 3 hours or until meat thermometer registers 130 degrees. In sauce pan, stir together cranberry sauce, brown sugar, burgundy, and mustard; simmer uncovered 5 minutes. During last 30 minutes baking time for ham, spoon half of cranberry glaze over ham. Pass remaining as a sauce.   *Serves 12*

SWEET POTATO CASSEROLE

1 60-ounce can sweet potato pieces, drained, reserving about 1 cup packing liquid
3/4 cup undiluted evaporated milk
3 tablespoons margarine, softened
dash salt
1/2 teaspoon grated orange peel
1/4 teaspoon cinnamon
1/4 scant teaspoon nutmeg
3/8 cup brown sugar, firmly packed
large size marshmallows

Put all ingredients, except marshmallows and reserved 1 cup packing liquid, in large mixer bowl and beat slowly, adding reserved liquid a little at a time, until desired consistency. (Keep in mind that the mixture will not thicken when cooked.) Discard any reserved liquid not used. Taste mixture for seasoning; adjust if desired. Place in greased 2-quart casserole. Cover and bake in 400 degree oven until hot and bubbling around the edges—about 30 minutes. Remove from oven, uncover, place marshmallows on top (almost touching one another) and return to oven. Bake, uncovered, until marshmallows are melted and lightly browned, about 5 to 8 minutes. Watch closely at this point. This can be mixed ahead and kept in refrigerator. Lengthen cooking time if the casserole is cold.   *Serves 12*

GREEN BEAN CASSEROLE

4 cans french style green beans
1 small can sliced water chestnuts
2 cans cream of chicken soup
1 stick margarine

2 chopped onions
2 cloves garlic
2 cups buttered bread crumbs

Drain canned french style green beans. Add water chestnuts and cream of mushroom soup. Melt margarine in pan and add chopped onion and cloves of garlic. Cook until soft. Add to bean mixture and place in casserole. Top with buttered bread crumbs. Bake for 30 minutes at 350 degrees.

Serves 12

HONEY-CORNMEAL BISCUITS

1 3/4 cups Bisquick baking mix
1/2 cup yellow cornmeal

1/2 cup milk
2 tablespoons honey

Heat oven to 450 degrees. Mix all together until dough forms; beat 30 seconds. Turn dough onto surface dusted with baking mix; gently roll in baking mix to coat. Shape into ball; knead 10 times. Roll 1/2" thick. Cut with 2" cutter dipped in baking mix. Bake on ungreased cookie sheet until golden brown, 8 to 10 minutes. Serve with additional honey or honey butter (recipe follows).
NOTE: You may make drop biscuits by dropping dough by rounded spoonfuls onto ungreased cookie sheet. Bake 10 to 12 minutes or until biscuits are golden brown.

Makes 12 biscuits

Honey Butter: Beat 1/2 cup butter, softened, 1/4 cup honey, and 1/2 teaspoon grated orange peel if desired, until fluffy.

BANANA SPLIT SQUARES

3 cups graham cracker crumbs
3 1/2 sticks melted margarine
2 cups powdered sugar
2 eggs
1 teaspoon vanilla
6 or 7 bananas
1 20-ounce can crushed pineapple, well drained
1 12-ounce container prepared whipped topping
1 cup chopped nuts
small jar maraschino cherries
1 cup lemon juice

For crust, combine 3 cups graham cracker crumbs and 1 1/2 sticks melted margarine. Press against bottom and sides of a 9x13 pan. Place 2 sticks softened margarine, sugar, eggs, and vanilla into mixer bowl. Beat 20 minutes with electric mixer and spread on crust. Slice bananas lengthwise or crosswise. Dip in lemon juice and arrange on batter. Spread pineapple on top of bananas. Spread whipped topping mix over pineapple. Sprinkle with nuts and sliced cherries. Chill several hours. Cut into small squares to serve. *Serves 12*

MOTHER'S DAY BRUNCH

Serves 6

Smoothie

Pineapple Casserole

Do-Ahead Sausage Souffle

Jalapeno Grits Casserole

Strawberry Bread

Brunch Bread

Apricot Nectar Cake

Shopping List

- 1 pound sausage links
- 1/2 pound bacon
- 16 eggs
- 2 1/4 cups milk
- 4 ounces grated Swiss or American cheese
- 16 ounces grated cheddar cheese
- 1 6-ounce roll Jalapeno pepper cheese
- 6 slices white bread
- 1 1/2 cups chopped pecans
- 1 package dry yeast
- 1 lemon cake mix
- 3 1/4 cups vegetable oil
- 3 cups sugar
- 1 cup powdered sugar
- 6 cups flour
- 1 teaspoon baking soda
- 1/2 teaspoon dry mustard
- 2 1/2 teaspoons salt
- dash paprika
- 1 teaspoon cinnamon
- 6 boxes frozen strawberries
- 4 small cans frozen orange juice
- 1 cup apricot nectar
- 1 cup grits
- 4 bananas
- 1 lemon
- 3 1/2 cups canned chunk pineapple
- 1 10 3/4-ounce can cream of mushroom soup

SMOOTHIE

4 small boxes frozen strawberries
4 bananas
4 small cans undiluted frozen orange juice

Partially thaw strawberries and orange juice. Mix in blender.

Serves 6

PINEAPPLE CASSEROLE

3 1/2 cups chunk pineapple
8 ounces grated cheddar cheese
1/3 cup sugar
1/3 cup flour

Drain pineapple. Add to juice, sugar, and flour, stirring until well mixed. Layer pineapple and cheese in casserole. Pour juice mixture over all. Bake at 300 degrees for 30 minutes.

Serves 6

DO-AHEAD SAUSAGE SOUFFLE

6 slices soft bread (cubed)
2 cups shredded cheddar cheese
1 pound sausage links cooked and cut in thirds
3 eggs
2 cups milk
1/2 teaspoon dry mustard
1 10 3/4-ounce can cream of mushroom soup

Spread bread evenly in bottom of 2-quart baking dish. Sprinkle cheese over bread. Arrange sausage on top. Beat eggs with 1 1/2 cups milk. Mix remaining 1/2 cup milk with mustard and soup. Pour egg mixture over layered bread, cheese, and sausage. Top casserole with soup mixture. Cover tightly. Refrigerate overnight. Place in cold oven. Set oven on 300 degrees; bake about one hour or until puffy and brown. Serve immediately.

Serves 6

JALAPENO GRITS CASSEROLE

1 cup grits
4 cups salted boiling water
1/2 stick butter or margarine
1 6-ounce roll Jalapeno pepper cheese

dash tabasco sauce
1/2 teaspoon salt
2 eggs, beaten
paprika

Cook grits in boiling salted water until thick. Add butter, Jalapeno cheese, tabasco sauce, and salt, mixing well. Fold eggs into grits; put into greased casserole. Sprinkle with paprika. Bake at 400 degrees uncovered for 30 minutes.

Serves 6

STRAWBERRY BREAD

3 cups flour
1 teaspoon salt
4 eggs, beaten
1 1/2 cups Wesson oil
2 cups sugar

1 teaspoon baking soda
1 teaspoon cinnamon
2 10-ounce packages frozen strawberries, thawed
1 1/2 cups pecans

Sift dry ingredients together. Combine eggs, oil, and strawberries. Add to dry ingredients and add pecans. Pour into two greased and floured loaf pans. Bake at 325 degrees about one hour. Cool on rack.
NOTE: This bread freezes well.

Serves 6

BRUNCH BREAD

1/2 pound bacon, cut into 1" pieces
1/4 cup vegetable oil (approximately)
1 package dry yeast
1/4 cup warm water
1/4 cup milk (scalded, then cooled)
1 1/2 teaspoons sugar
1 teaspoon salt
3 eggs
2 3/4 cups flour
1/2 cup diced Swiss or American cheese

Fry bacon until crisp, drain, reserving bacon fat. Add enough vegetable oil to fat to measure 1/2 cup. Set bacon and fat-oil mixture aside. Dissolve yeast in warm water in large mixing bowl. Add milk, sugar, salt, reserved fat-oil mixture, eggs and 1 1/2 cups flour. Beat 10 minutes on medium speed. Stir in remaining flour with spoon until smooth. Cover and let rise in warm place until double (about 1 hour). Punch down batter; gently work in cheese and reserved fried bacon until well distributed. Shape into ball. Place in greased 8- or 9-inch pie pan or 9- or 10-inch ovenproof skillet. Let rise until double (about 1 hour). Heat oven to 375 degrees and bake 30 minutes. Remove from pan and cool on wire rack.

Serves 6

APRICOT NECTAR CAKE

1 18.5-ounce lemon cake mix
4 eggs
1/2 cup sugar
3/4 cup vegetable oil
1 cup apricot nectar

Grease and flour tube pan. Mix all ingredients thoroughly. Bake at 325 degrees for 1 hour.

Glaze with the following recipe while still hot: 1 cup powdered sugar and juice of 1 lemon. Mix ingredients and pour over hot cake. Serve cake when cool.

Serves 6

MEMORIAL DAY LUNCH

Serves 8

Collegiate Tea Punch
Spinach Cottage Cheese Salad
Talerine
Onion-Cheese French Bread
Ice Cream Sundae Dessert

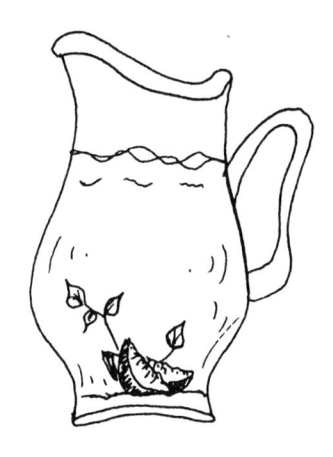

Shopping List

2 oranges *or* 2 lemons
1 package fresh spinach
1 head green lettuce
1 small red onion
2 1/2 medium white onions
3/4 pound fresh mushrooms
2 medium bell peppers
1/4 cup chopped green onion
1 pound + 3 ounces cheddar cheese
3/4 cup Swiss cheese
1 cup cottage cheese
1/4 cup margarine
1/2 cup butter
1 quart vanilla ice cream
1 8-ounce container prepared whipped topping
1/2 pound bacon
2 pounds ground beef
1 16-ounce loaf French bread
24 Oreo cookies
6 teaspoons tea leaves
1 package wide egg noodles

1/2 cup mint leaves *or* 1/4 teaspoon mint extract
1/2 cup lemon juice
1 1/4 cup white vinegar
2 cups vegetable oil
2 cups orange juice
1/2 cup mayonnaise
1 large can evaporated milk
1 teaspoon vanilla
1 1/2 teaspoon dry mustard
1 1/2 teaspoon salt
4 1/3 cups sugar
1 cup pecans
2 squares unsweetened baking chocolate
1 1/2 tablespoons poppy seed
2 small cans cream style corn
1 can ripe olives
2 cans tomato soup
16 maraschino cherries with stems
2 pints ginger ale

COLLEGIATE TEA PUNCH

2 cups boiling water
6 teaspoons tea leaves
1/2 cup crushed mint leaves *or*
   1/4 teaspoon mint extract

1 1/3 cups sugar
2 cups orange juice
1/2 cup lemon juice
2 pints chilled ginger ale

Pour boiling water over tea and mint leaves or mint extract. Steep for five minutes. Strain. Add sugar and stir until dissolved. Cool. Add fruit juice and additional sugar if desired. Pour over ice in eight tall glasses and fill glasses with ginger ale. Garnish with orange and lemon slices.
Serves 8

SPINACH COTTAGE CHEESE SALAD

1 package fresh spinach
1 head lettuce
   small red onion
3/4 pound fresh mushrooms
3/4 cup Swiss cheese
1 cup drained cottage cheese
1/2 pound bacon, fried and crumbled

Dressing:
1 1/2 cups vegetable oil
1 1/4 cups white vinegar
3/4 cup sugar
1 1/2 tablespoons poppy seeds
1 1/2 tablespoons minced onion
1 1/2 teaspoons salt
1 1/2 teaspoons dry mustard

Combine salad ingredients just before serving, add dressing and toss.
Serves 8

TALERINE

2 pounds ground beef
1/2 cup vegetable oil
2 medium onions
2 medium bell peppers
2 small cans cream style corn
1 can sliced ripe olives
1 package wide egg noodles
2 cans tomato soup
1 pound cheddar cheese

Brown beef in vegetable oil. Add onion and green pepper, cooking until soft. Add corn and olives. Cook egg noodles 7 minutes and add to first mixture. Mix one can soup into mixture. Pour mixture into a casserole dish. Pour remaining can of soup on top of mixture. Top with grated cheese. Bake in 350 degree oven for 30 minutes or until brown.

Serves 8

ONION-CHEESE FRENCH BREAD

1/4 cup margarine, softened
3/4 cup (3 ounces) shredded cheddar cheese
1/2 cup mayonnaise
1/4 cup chopped green onions
1 16-ounce loaf French bread

Combine first four ingredients; mix well. Slice bread in half lengthwise. Spread cheese mixture on bread. Broil 6 inches from heat 2 minutes or until bubbly.

Serves 8 to 10

Tip: Try this recipe for a crowd. Spread topping on bread ahead of time, tightly wrap, and refrigerate. Unwrap and broil right before serving.

ICE CREAM SUNDAE DESSERT

24 Oreo cookies
1 stick butter
1 quart vanilla ice cream
1 8-ounce container prepared whipped topping
1 cup pecans
16 maraschino cherries with stems

2 squares unsweetened baking chocolate
2 cups sugar
1 large can evaporated milk
1 teaspoon vanilla

Grease 9x13 Pyrex dish. Crush Oreo cookies. Melt butter. Stir cookies into butter and press into dish; freeze. Spread vanilla ice cream on top of cookies; freeze. Top with the following fudge sauce which has been previously made and cooled. Cook unsweetened baking chocolate, sugar, and milk to boiling until thick. When cool, add vanilla and spread on ice cream; freeze. Spread prepared whipped topping, sprinkle nuts, and position cherry for each serving in that order on top of fudge sauce. Freeze.

Serves 8 to 10

FATHER'S DAY BARBECUE

Serves 8

Punch with a "Punch"

Tex-Mex Dip

Backyard Coleslaw

Brisket

Rice and Broccoli Casserole

Snappy Carrots

Monkey Bread II

PTA Dessert

Shopping List

- 1 46-ounce can pineapple juice
- 1 46-ounce can Hawaiian punch
- 1 12-ounce can frozen lemonade
- 1 12-ounce can frozen orange juice
- 1 32-ounce bottle ginger ale
- 1 1/4 cups lemon juice
- 1 8-10 pound beef brisket
- 2 1/2 cups milk
- 1 1/2 cups sour cream
- 1 8-ounce package sharp cheddar cheese
- 1 8-ounce package grated cheddar cheese
- 2 8-ounce packages cream cheese
- 1 cup whipping cream
- 4 teaspoons butter
- 1 3/4 cups margarine
- 2 eggs
- 4 tablespoons prepared horseradish
- 1 12-ounce container + 1 cup whipped cream topping
- 1 package frozen broccoli
- 1 can cream of celery soup
- 1 can cream of mushroom soup
- 1 can cream of chicken soup
- 4 cups sugar
- 1 cup powdered sugar
- 7 cups flour
- 1 3/4 teaspoons salt
- 1 teaspoon Lowry's seasoned salt
- dash white pepper
- 1/2 teaspoon pepper
- 1 teaspoon onion or garlic salt
- 1 teaspoon whole celery seed
- Adolph's meat tenderizer
- 2 packages dry yeast
- 1 teaspoon celery salt
- 1 small box instant vanilla pudding
- 1 small box instant chocolate pudding
- 1 jar chocolate sprinkles
- 1/2 cup chopped pecans
- 2 tablespoons Dijon-style prepared mustard

Shopping List, continued

- 6 ounces liquid smoke barbecue sauce
- 8 tablespoons Worcestershire sauce
- 1 1/2 cups mayonnaise
- 7 saltine crackers
- large round tortilla chips
- 1 package taco seasoning mix
- 2 10.5-ounce cans plain Jalapeno flavored bean dip
- 2 3 1/3-ounce cans pitted ripe olives
- 1 1/2 cups rice
- 1 large onion
- 4 bananas
- 3 medium size ripe avocados
- 2 bunches green onions
- 3 medium size tomatoes
- 6 cups grated cabbage
- 20 carrots
- 1 medium apple
- 2 lemons

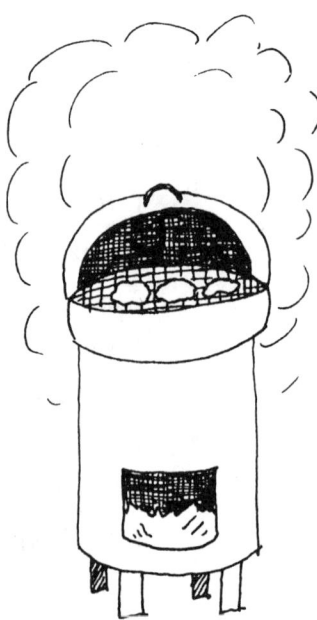

PUNCH WITH A "PUNCH"

1 23-ounce can pineapple juice
1 23-ounce can Hawaiian punch
1 6-ounce can frozen lemonade
1 6-ounce can frozen orange juice
1 16-ounce bottle ginger ale
4 bananas
1/8 cup lemon juice
3 cups water
1 1/2 cups sugar

Blend bananas in blender with lemon juice. Mix in all ingredients except ginger ale. Freeze mixture in one-quart containers. Remove mixture two hours before serving from freezer. Add one bottle ginger ale to two quarts frozen punch.

Serves 25

TEX-MEX DIP

3 medium size ripe avocados
2 tablespoons lemon juice
1/2 teaspoon salt
1/4 teaspoon pepper
1 cup (8-ounces) sour cream
1/2 cup mayonnaise
1 1.25-ounce package taco seasoning mix
2 10.5-ounce cans plain jalapeno flavored bean dip
1 large bunch green onions with tops, chopped (1 cup)
3 medium size tomatoes, cored, halved, and coarsely chopped (2 cups)
2 3.5-ounce cans pitted ripe olives, drained, coarsely chopped
1 8-ounce package sharp cheddar cheese, grated
large round tortilla chips

Peel, pit, and mash avocados in a medium size bowl with lemon juice, salt, and pepper. Combine sour cream, mayonnaise, and taco seasoning mix in bowl. To assemble, spread bean dip on a large shallow serving platter; top with seasoned avocado mixture; layer with sour cream-taco mixture. Sprinkle with chopped onions, tomatoes, and olives; cover with shredded cheese. Serve chilled or at room temperature with round tortilla chips.

Serves 8

BACKYARD COLESLAW

6 cups thinly sliced cabbage
1 cup thinly sliced carrots
1/2 cup sliced green onion
1 cup whipping cream
1/2 cup sour cream
1/3 cup fresh lemon juice
3 tablespoons sugar

2 tablespoons Dijon-style prepared mustard
1 teaspoon whole celery seed
1/4 teaspoon salt
1/4 teaspoon pepper
1 cup chopped red apple

Combine cabbage, carrots and onion in a large mixing bowl; cover and chill. Just before serving, combine whipping cream, sour cream, lemon juice, sugar, mustard, celery seed, salt, and pepper in a small chilled mixing bowl. Beat until almost stiff. Stir apple into cabbage mixture. Stir whipped cream mixture into cabbage mixture; toss gently. Serve at once.

Serves 8

BRISKET

1 8 to 10 pound brisket
  Adolph's meat tenderizer
  Lawry's seasoned salt
  celery salt

onion or garlic salt
6 ounces bottled liquid smoke
8 tablespoons worcestershire sauce

Trim fat from brisket. Season on both sides with meat tenderizer, seasoned salt, celery salt, and onion salt (sparingly). Put in pan with cover. Cover with liquid smoke and worcestershire sauce. Set in refrigerator for 24 hours. Bake at 225 degrees for 8 hours. Refrigerate. Remove grease. Slice; reheat in heavy foil. Use drippings for sauce.

Serves 8

RICE AND BROCCOLI CASSEROLE

1 1/2 cups rice, cooked as package directs
1 package frozen broccoli, cooked as package directs
1 can cream of celery soup
1 can cream of mushroom soup
1 can cream of chicken soup
1/2 pound grated cheddar cheese

Combine drained rice and broccoli with soups. Top with cheese. Bake at 350 degrees until cheese is melted—about 20 minutes.

Serves 8

SNAPPY CARROTS

9 cups sliced carrots
1 cup mayonnaise
4 tablespoons chopped onions
4 tablespoons prepared horseradish
1/2 teaspoon salt
dash white pepper
1/2 cup crushed saltine crackers (7)
4 teaspoons butter, melted

Cook carrots in a small amount of salted water until tender. Drain and place carrots in a lightly greased 1-quart baking dish. Combine mayonnaise, onion, horseradish, salt, and pepper. Stir into carrots. Mix crushed crackers with butter. Sprinkle on carrots. Bake 30 minutes at 350 degrees. This may be prepared ahead of time and refrigerated.

Serves 8

MONKEY BREAD II

2 packages yeast
1/4 cup warm water
3/4 cup margarine
1/2 teaspoon salt

1/2 cup sugar
2 eggs, slightly beaten
5 to 6 cups flour
1 cup boiling water

Dissolve yeast in warm water. Combine shortening, sugar, and salt in large mixing bowl. Pour in boiling water. Stir until dissolved. Cool. Add eggs and yeast mixture. Add 2 cups flour; beat until smooth. Add remaining flour, 1 cup at a time until a medium dough is formed. Knead slightly. Let rise until double in bulk (about 1 1/2 hours). Roll into rectangle 1/2" thick. Cut into 1" squares. Dip in melted butter. Throw into tube pan. Let rise until double. Bake at 375 degrees until golden brown (30 to 40 minutes). Pour 1 stick melted butter over bread while still in pan. Serve hot.

Serves 8

PTA DESSERT

1 cup flour
1/2 cup margarine
1/2 cup pecans, chopped
1 8-ounce package cream cheese
1 cup prepared whipped topping
1 cup powdered sugar
1 small box instant vanilla pudding

1 small box instant chocolate pudding
2 1/2 cups cold milk
1 container prepared whipped topping
1 jar chocolate sprinkles

Combine flour, margarine, and nuts and press into 9x12 pan. Bake 15 minutes at 375 degrees. Mix and spread over cooled crust: cream cheese, prepared whipped topping, and powdered sugar that have been thoroughly combined. Mix vanilla and chocolate pudding with milk according to directions on pudding box. Spread on top of cream cheese mixture. Top dessert with prepared whipped topping and chocolate sprinkles in that order.

Serves 8 generously

FOURTH OF JULY FIESTA

Serves 6

Mock Margarita

Sangria Punch

Fiesta Dip

Chili Beef Dip

Guacamole Dip

Tortilla Soup

Mexican Salad

Texas Casserole

Corn Marinate

Whipped Cream Praline

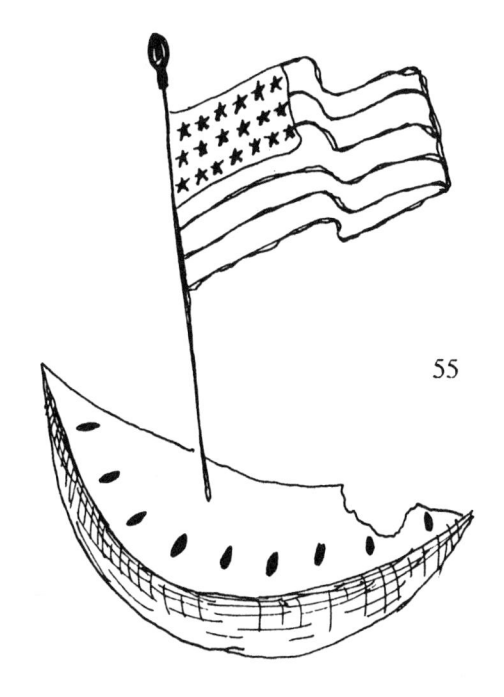

Shopping List

1 6-ounce can frozen lemonade concentrate
1 6-ounce can frozen limeade concentrate
1 quart cranberry juice cocktail
1 cup grape juice
6 large marshmallows
1/2 cup dark brown sugar
2 cups white sugar
1/2 cup powdered sugar
1 teaspoon vanilla
    coarse salt
3 teaspoons salt
    dash red pepper
3 dashes black pepper
1/8 teaspoon chili powder
4 tablespoons ground onion
1 bay leaf
2 teaspoons cumin
2 teaspoons dry mustard
2 8-ounce packages cream cheese
4 ounces cheddar *or* Monterey Jack cheese, grated

1 pound longhorn cheese, grated
1 pound (4 cups) sharp cheddar cheese, grated
1/2 cup real butter
1/4 cup margarine
4 tablespoons cream
1/2 cup whipping cream
2 eggs
2 cooked chicken breasts
2 cups diced cooked chicken
1/4 cup + 2 tablespoons vegetable oil
3 tablespoons white Karo syrup
1/2 cup cider vinegar
4 teaspoons enchilada sauce
2/3 cup ketchup
6 tablespoons French dressing
1 bottle Kraft catalina dressing
1 pint club soda
1 lime
1 lemon
1 orange
4 stalks celery

Shopping List, continued

3 large onions
1 green pepper
4 tomatoes
4 ripe avocados
4 green onions
4 cloves garlic
1 head lettuce
1/4 pound fresh mushrooms
1 10-ounce can Rotel tomatoes with green chilies
1 can white shoepeg corn
1 can yellow whole kernel corn
1 small jar chopped pimentos
1 10.5-ounce can cream of chicken soup
1 10 1/2-ounce can cream of mushroom soup
1 jar maraschino cherries
1 can chili beef soup
1 can cheddar cheese soup
1 large can tomatoes
1 quart + 1 cup chicken stock
1 quart beef stock
1 6-ounce can tomato sauce
1 15-ounce can Ranch style beans
2 large packages corn tortillas
1 large bag of your favorite chips
2 king size packages Fritos
1 large bag tostados
2 cups pecans

MOCK MARGARITA

1 6-ounce can frozen lemonade concentrate, thawed
1 6-ounce can frozen limeade concentrate, thawed
1/2 cup powdered sugar
2 egg whites
3 cups crushed ice
1 pint (2 cups) club soda
lime slices
coarse salt

In 2-quart non-metal container, combine lemonade, limeade, powdered sugar, egg whites, and crushed ice. Mix well. Cover and freeze, stirring occasionally. Remove 30 minutes before serving. To serve, rub rim of glass with lime slice and dip rim in coarse salt. Spoon one cup slush mixture into blender and add 1/2 cup club soda. Blend until frothy. Pour mixture into glasses rimmed with salt.

Serves 6

SANGRIA PUNCH

1 quart cranberry juice cocktail
1 cup grape juice
cracked ice
lemon slices
orange slices
small jar maraschino cherries

Combine cranberry juice cocktail and grape juice; chill. At serving time, pour mixture over cracked ice in glasses. Garnish each with lemon and orange slices and a maraschino cherry.

Serves 6

FIESTA DIP

2 8-ounce packages cream cheese
4 tablespoons cream or milk
6 tablespoons french dressing
2/3 cup ketchup
3 tablespoons ground onion
1 teaspoon salt
red pepper to taste

Combine ingredients and refrigerate. Serve with Fritos.

Serves 6

CHILI BEEF DIP

1 can chili beef soup
1 can cheddar cheese soup

Combine soups and heat in saucepan. Serve warm with your favorite chips.

Serves 6

GUACAMOLE DIP

3 ripe avocados
2 tomatoes
1 small onion
4 teaspoons enchilada sauce
salt
pepper

Combine ingredients in blender, adding salt and pepper to taste. Serve with tostados.

Serves 6

TORTILLA SOUP

1 large onion, chopped
1 large can tomatoes, drained
2 tablespoons oil
1 corn tortilla, chopped
4 cloves garlic, minced
1/8 teaspoon chili powder
1 bay leaf
2 teaspoons ground cumin
1 quart chicken stock
1 quart beef stock
1 6-ounce can tomato soup
2 cooked chicken breasts, chopped
4 ounces cheddar or Monterey Jack cheese, grated
1 avocado, diced
2 cups thinly sliced strips of fried tortillas

Blend onion and tomatoes until smooth. Saute in oil the corn tortilla, garlic, adding chili powder. Heat to a boil: bay leaf, cumin, chicken stock, and beef stock; stir in onion and tomato mixture, adding tomato sauce. Also add corn tortilla, garlic, and chili powder. Salt and pepper to taste. Simmer over medium heat for 30 minutes. Strain through a coarse strainer. May be made ahead and reheated when ready to serve. To serve, put warm cooked chicken, cheese, avocado, and crisp tortillas in bowls. Heat the broth to a boil and ladle over chicken.

Serves 6

MEXICAN SALAD

1 head lettuce, cut or broken for salad
2 tomatoes, diced
1/2 onion, finely chopped
1 pound longhorn cheese, grated
1 15-ounce can Ranch style beans, rinsed and drained
1 bottle Kraft catalina dressing
1 package king size Fritos

Rinse chilled beans. Combine everything except Fritos. Chill for 1 hour with dressing. Before serving, crush Fritos and stir into salad. Serve immediately.

Serves 6

TEXAS CASSEROLE

1 cup diced onion
1/4 pound fresh or canned mushrooms
1/4 cup margarine
1 10 1/2-ounce can cream of mushroom soup
1 10 1/2-ounce can cream of chicken soup
1 pound (4 cups) grated sharp cheddar cheese
1 10-ounce can Rotel tomatoes with green chilies
1 cup chicken broth
1 8-ounce package soft tortillas
2 cups diced cooked chicken

Saute onion and mushrooms in margarine. Add soups, tomatoes, garlic, and chili powder. Place the tortillas in chicken broth for 10 minutes. Line a casserole dish with the tortillas. Fill the remainder of the dish with alternate layers of diced chicken, sauce, and cheese. Bake at 350 degrees for 30 minutes.

Serves 6

CORN MARINATE

1 can white shoepeg corn
1 can yellow whole kernel corn
4 stalks celery
4 green onions
1 green pepper
1 small can chopped pimento
1/2 cup cider vinegar
1/4 cup oil
1/3 cup sugar
2 teaspoons dry mustard
pepper

Drain the corn. Chop celery, green onions, green pepper; add to corn. Add pimento to corn and mix. Mix together vinegar, oil, sugar, dry mustard, and salt and pepper to taste. Pour over corn and marinate at least 6 hours.

Serves 6

WHIPPED CREAM PRALINE

3 tablespoons white Karo syrup
1 1/2 cups white sugar
1/2 cup dark brown sugar
   pinch of salt
1/2 cup whipping cream

1/2 cup real butter
6 large marshmallows
1 teaspoon vanilla
2 cups frozen pecans

Cook first five ingredients to soft ball stage using a candy thermometer. Add real butter and marshmallows, cut in pieces. Mix until marshmallows and butter are melted. Set in a bowl of cold water for 1 to 2 minutes. Add 2 cups frozen pecans. Drop spoonfuls of mixture on wax paper. You may need help as these set up quickly.

Makes 3 dozen pralines

LABOR DAY BUFFET

Serves 12

Jello Punch

Layered Broccoli Salad

Candied Ham Loaf with Fluffy Mustard Sauce

Baked Beans

Lemon Herb Potatoes

Tupperware Bread

Almond Joy Cake

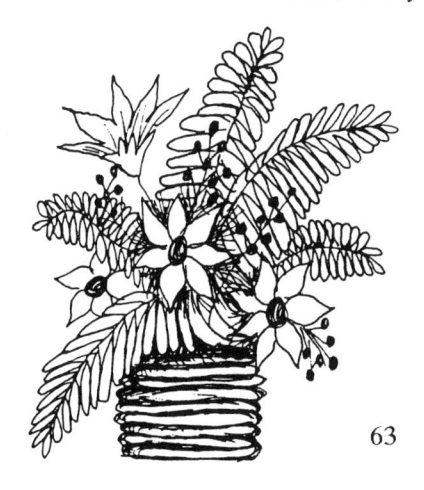

Shopping List

28 slices bacon
2 cups shredded cheddar cheese
2 pounds ground cooked ham
1 pound ground beef
1 tablespoon horseradish
1/2 pint whipping cream
3 1/2 cups milk
8 eggs
2 1/2 cups + 5 tablespoons margarine
1 tablespoon oil
1/2 cup lemon juice
1 46-ounce can pineapple juice
1 3-ounce package cherry jello
1 quart ginger ale
9 cups whole wheat flour
2 cups brown sugar
2 3/4 cups white sugar
2 1/4 teaspoons salt
1/4 teaspoon white pepper
1 tablespoon dry mustard
1 teaspoon ground cloves

2 teaspoons grated lemon peel
1 teaspoon dried dill weed
2 tablespoons parsley
dash paprika
1 chocolate pudding cake mix
ingredients for cake mix
24 large marshmallows
1 cup evaporated milk
1 14-ounce bag coconut
1 1/2 cups milk chocolate chips
2 packages dry yeast
1 cup chopped almonds
1 cup mayonnaise
3 tablespoons prepared mustard
1 cup ketchup
6 tablespoons red wine vinegar
2 cups bread crumbs
4 16-ounce cans pork and beans
2 heads broccoli
3 small onions
6 large Irish potatoes
2 cloves garlic

JELLO PUNCH

1 3-ounce package cherry jello
1 cup hot water
1 cup sugar
3 1/2 cups cold water

1 46-ounce can pineapple juice
1/2 cup lemon juice
1 quart ginger ale

Dissolve jello in hot water; add sugar, then remaining water. Add pineapple juice and lemon juice. Freeze mixture. When ready to serve, add ginger ale to frozen ingredients. The mixture should be slushy.

Serves 12

LAYERED BROCCOLI SALAD

2 heads broccoli, cut fine
2 cups shredded cheddar cheese
2 small chopped onions
16 crisp slices bacon, crumbled

1 cup mayonnaise
1/2 cup sugar
4 tablespoons red wine vinegar

Layer broccoli, onion, and bacon. Top with cheddar cheese. Before serving, add dressing by mixing mayonnaise, sugar, and red wine vinegar together.

Serves 12

CANDIED HAM LOAF

2 pounds ground cooked ham
1 pound ground beef
2 cups bread crumbs
1 cup milk
2 eggs

1/2 teaspoon salt
1 teaspoon dry mustard
1/2 cup brown sugar
1 teaspoon ground cloves

Combine ham, beef, bread crumbs, and milk. Blend in eggs. Mix remaining ingredients. In bottom of baking dish combine brown sugar and cloves. Put meat on top. Bake an hour at 350 degrees. Serve with fluffy mustard sauce (recipe follows).

Serves 12

FLUFFY MUSTARD SAUCE

2 egg yolks, beaten
1 tablespoon sugar
3 tablespoons prepared mustard
2 tablespoons vinegar
1 tablespoon water

3/4 teaspoon salt
1 tablespoon margarine
1 tablespoon horseradish
1/2 pint cream, whipped

Add sugar, mustard, vinegar, water, and salt to egg yolks; mix well. Cook over hot (not boiling) water, stirring until thick. Blend in margarine and horseradish. Cool. Add cream. Serve with Candied Ham Loaf.

Makes 1 1/2 cups

BAKED BEANS

4 16-ounce or 18-ounce cans pork and beans
1 1/2 cups brown sugar
2 teaspoons dry mustard
12 slices bacon cut in pieces
1 cup ketchup

Put two cans of beans in greased 13 1/2x8 3/4x1 3/4" casserole. Mix brown sugar and mustard. Sprinkle 1/2 of that mixture over beans. Pour remaining beans on sugar mixture. Sprinkle other half of sugar mixture over beans. Sprinkle uncooked bacon over top of sugar mixture. Add ketchup over bacon. Bake at 325 degrees uncovered for 2 1/2 hours.

Serves 12

LEMON HERB POTATOES

6 large baking potatoes
2/3 cup chopped onion
2 cloves garlic, minced
4 tablespoons margarine
1 cup hot skim milk
2 teaspoons grated lemon peel
1/4 teaspoon white pepper
1 teaspoon dried dill weed
2 tablespoons finely chopped parsley
paprika

Bake potatoes. Let potatoes cool so you can handle them. While potatoes are cooling, saute onion and garlic in margarine until tender. Cut potatoes in half; scoop out potato insides, being careful to keep skins from breaking. Mash potatoes. Beat in sauteed onion mixture, hot skim milk, lemon peel, and pepper. Mix in dill weed and parsley. Pile mashed potato mixture into skins. Sprinkle with paprika. Bake at 400 degrees about 30 minutes or until lightly browned.

Serves 12

TUPPERWARE BREAD

9 cups whole wheat flour
4 eggs
1/2 cup sugar
2 packages dry yeast

1 1/2 cups milk
1 1/2 cups water
1 teaspoon salt
2 sticks margarine

Put flour in large Tupperware bowl. Make well in bottom. Beat eggs with fork; add sugar mixed with yeast, scalded milk cooled with water, and salt. Pour liquid mixture into flour well but do not mix. Seal, burp bowl (remove air), and set bowl in warm water for 30 minutes. Seal will pop off when ready. Then add 2 sticks melted margarine. Mix well. Seal, burp bowl, and return to warm water for another 30 to 40 minutes. When seal has popped off the second time, knead 15 to 20 times and divide and shape into 3 to 4 loaves. Place in greased loaf pans. Let rise 15 to 20 minutes—no more. Bake at 375 degrees for 30 minutes. Brush top of bread with melted butter and cool on wire racks.

Makes 3 - 4 loaves

ALMOND JOY CAKE

1 chocolate pudding cake mix
24 large marshmallows
1 cup evaporated milk
1 cup sugar
1 14-ounce bag of coconut

1 stick margarine
1 tablespoon oil
1 1/2 cups milk chocolate chips
1 cup almonds

Prepare cake mix as directed on box. Pour cake into a large sheet cake pan and bake at 350 degrees until toothpick inserted comes out clean. While cake is baking melt marshmallows mixed with evaporated milk and sugar. Add coconut. When cake is done, punch holes in hot cake with wooden spoon handle and pour coconut mixture over cake. Then prepare icing by mixing and bringing to a boil the following ingredients: 1 1/2 cups sugar, 1/2 cup evaporated milk, 1 stick margarine, 1 tablespoon oil. Remove ingredients from heat and add 1 1/2 cups chocolate chips and 1 cup chopped almonds that have been salted and toasted in the oven. Spread on cake over coconut mixture.

Serves 12

HALLOWEEN EVENING DESSERT BUFFET

Serves 24

Hot Orange Cider
White Grape Juice Spritzer
Pumpkin Cake
Pineapple Upside Down Cake
Milky Way Cake
Gingerbread Cake with Lemon Sauce
Brandy Cream Pie
Easy Millionaire Pie
Date Nut Pie
Kahlua Crunch
Chocolate Layer Squares
Hello Dollies
Cherry Salad
Glazed Fruit Salad

Shopping List

2 12-ounce cans frozen orange juice concentrate
8 12-ounce cartons prepared whipped topping
38 eggs
4 cups margarine
7 1/2 cups butter
1 cup milk
2 1/2 cups buttermilk
9 ounces cream cheese
3 pints sour cream
3 quarts apple cider
2 bottles white catawba grape juice
1 32-ounce bottle club soda
16 medium Milky Way candy bars
1 4-ounce German sweet chocolate bar
2 cans pumpkin
1 large can sliced pineapple (10 slices)
2 12-ounce cans evaporated milk
2 packages yellow cake mix
4 1/2 cups brown sugar

3 cups cake flour
20 cups white sugar
10 cups flour
3 tablespoons cornstarch
4 teaspoons pumpkin spice
3 3/4 teaspoons salt
8 1/2 teaspoons baking powder
2 1/2 teaspoons soda
24 long sticks cinnamon
1/4 teaspoon powdered cinnamon
2 1/4 teaspoons ginger
9 1/4 teaspoons vanilla
4 1/2 teaspoons grated lemon rind
4 teaspoons lemon flavoring
6 cans sweetened condensed milk
2 6-ounce + 1 3-ounce packages instant vanilla pudding mix
2 3/4 cups powdered sugar
4 1/3 cups flaked coconut
4 squares unsweetened chocolate
24 cupcake liners

Shopping List, continued

- 1 cup chocolate chips *or* butterscotch chips
- 2 cans cherry pie filling
- 2 cups miniature marshmallows
- 1 1/2 cups molasses
- 23 tablespoons lemon juice
- 3 baked 10-inch pie shells
- 2 1/2 cups graham cracker crumbs
- 3 boxes Zwieback
- 3 cups vanilla wafer crumbs
- 3 cups chopped dates
- 4 cups maraschino cherries
- 4 11-ounce cans mandarin oranges
- 8 20-ounce cans chunk pineapple
- 42 ounces canned crushed pineapple
- 2 cups almonds
- 17 cups chopped pecans
- 2 oranges
- 1 lemon
- 1 lime
- 12 large bananas
- 4 1/2 ounces brandy
- 6 teaspoons Kahlua

HOT ORANGE CIDER

2 12-ounce cans frozen orange juice concentrate
3 quarts apple cider
2 oranges cut into 24 slices

Prepare orange juice as directed on can. Heat orange juice and apple cider just to boiling over low heat. Pour about 2 cups orange juice mixture into each mug. Top with orange slice. Garnish with stick cinnamon if desired.

Serves 24

WHITE GRAPE JUICE SPRITZER

2 24-ounce bottles white catawba grape juice, chilled
1 32-ounce bottle club soda, chilled
1 lemon, sliced
1 lime, sliced

In large non-metal pitcher or punch bowl, combine grape juice and club soda. Garnish with lemon and lime slices. Serve immediately.

Serves 24

PUMPKIN CAKE

1 can pumpkin
1 12-ounce can evaporated milk
3 eggs
1/2 cup brown sugar
1/2 cup white sugar
1/4 teaspoon salt
2 teaspoons pumpkin spice
1 yellow cake mix
1/4 cup margarine
1 cup chopped pecans
1 carton prepared whipped topping

Mix and pour into 13x9 pan first seven ingredients. Sprinkle yellow cake mix on top. Drizzle on top of cake mix, 1/4 cup margarine. Sprinkle on top chopped pecans. Serve with whipped topping.

Serves 12

PINEAPPLE UPSIDE DOWN CAKE

1/2 cup butter
2/3 cup brown sugar
5 slices pineapple
1 egg
1 1/2 cups white sugar
1 1/2 cups cake flour

2 teaspoons baking powder
1/4 teaspoon salt
1/2 teaspoon vanilla
1/2 teaspoon lemon flavoring
1/3 cup milk

Melt 3 tablespoons butter in 9x9x2-inch pan. Add brown sugar and blend. Place pineapple slices in sugar. Cream remaining butter and white sugar. Add egg and beat well. Add vanilla and lemon flavoring. Sift flour, baking powder, and salt and add to mixture, stirring well. Bake at 350 degrees on an upper shelf in oven.
    NOTE: Prepare two recipes to serve 24 people.

MILKY WAY CAKE

8 medium size Milky Way bars
1 cup margarine
2 cups sugar
4 eggs

2 1/2 cups flour
1/2 teaspoon soda
1 1/4 cups buttermilk
1 cup chopped pecans

Melt Milky Way bars and one stick margarine over low heat. Cream sugar and one stick margarine; add eggs. Sift flour and soda. Add alternately with buttermilk. Add Milky Way mixture and nuts. Bake in bundt pan at 325 degrees for 1 hour and 10 minutes.
    NOTE: Prepare two recipes to serve 24 people.

GINGERBREAD

1/2 cup boiling water
1/2 cup margarine
1/2 cup brown sugar
1/2 cup molasses
1 egg, beaten
1 1/2 cups flour

1/2 teaspoon salt
1/2 teaspoon baking powder
1/2 teaspoon soda
3/4 teaspoon ginger
3/4 teaspoon cinnamon

Pour boiling water over margarine. Add brown sugar, molasses, egg, and flour sifted with salt, baking powder, soda, ginger, and cinnamon. Beat until smooth. Bake in greased 8-inch square pan in 350 degree oven for 35 minutes. Cool in pan. Top with warm Lemon Sauce (recipe follows).
NOTE: Prepare three recipes to serve 24 people.

LEMON SAUCE

1/2 cup sugar
1 tablespoon cornstarch
1 cup water
2 tablespoons butter

1/2 teaspoon grated lemon rind
1 1/2 tablespoons lemon juice
1/8 teaspoon salt

Combine sugar, cornstarch, and water, stirring constantly over low heat. When sauce thickens (in about 5 minutes), remove from heat and stir in remaining ingredients. Excellent served warm on gingerbread.
NOTE: Prepare three recipes to serve 24 people.

BRANDY CREAM PIE

1 box Zwieback crackers (in infant section of grocery store)
1/4 cup powdered sugar
6 tablespoons butter
dash powdered cinnamon
3 3-ounce packages cream cheese
2 eggs
1 cup white sugar
1 teaspoon lemon peel
1 1/2 ounces brandy
1 pint sour cream
2 teaspoons vanilla extract
8 teaspoons sugar

For the crust, crush enough Zwieback to make 1 1/2 cups fine crumbs. Mix them with powdered sugar, butter, and cinnamon. Press mixture evenly on bottom and sides of a 9-inch pie plate. Chill. For the filling, put into a blender or beat with an electric mixer until very smooth: cream cheese, eggs, sugar, lemon peel, and brandy. Pour the mixture into the pie shell and bake in a preheated 300 degree oven for 30 minutes. The filling should be almost firm, but may be a little jiggly in the center. It will firm up in the refrigerator. Remove pie from oven and cool. Spread with 1 pint sour cream which has been mixed with 2 teaspoons vanilla and 8 teaspoons sugar. Return pie to 250 degree oven for 10 minutes. Cool and refrigerate for at least 4 hours. Any remaining crumbs may be sprinkled over pie before second baking.
    NOTE: Prepare three recipes to serve 24 people.

EASY MILLIONAIRE PIE

1 can sweetened condensed milk
6 tablespoons lemon juice
1 8-ounce can crushed pineapple, drained thoroughly
1 cup chopped pecans
1 large carton prepared whipped topping
1 baked 10-inch pie shell

Mix all ingredients; fold in prepared whipped topping. Pour into baked pie shell. Chill at least 1 hour.
    NOTE: Prepare three recipes to serve 24 people.

DATE NUT PIE

1 cup vanilla wafer crumbs
1 teaspoon baking powder
1/4 teaspoon salt
3 egg whites

1 cup sugar
1 cup chopped dates
1 cup chopped pecans
1 cup whipped topping

Combine crumbs, baking powder, and salt. Beat egg whites with sugar until stiff. Fold egg whites into crumb mixture, then fold in dates, nuts, and vanilla. Turn into greased 9-inch pie plate. Bake at 350 degrees for 25 to 30 minutes. Cool and serve with whipped topping.
NOTE: Prepare three recipes to serve 24 people.

KAHLUA CRUNCH

Crust:
1 cup graham cracker crumbs
1/2 cup coconut
1/3 cup butter, melted
1/4 cup brown sugar

Filling:
1 1/4 cups butter, softened
1 cup sugar
1 square unsweetened chocolate, melted
1 teaspoon vanilla extract

2 teaspoons Kahlua
2 eggs
1 cup almonds, toasted and chopped
1 cup whipped topping

Preheat oven to 350 degrees. To make crust, combine graham cracker crumbs, coconut, melted butter, and brown sugar. Press into 9-inch pie plate. Bake 10 minutes. Cool. Break crust into small pieces. Sprinkle crust into 12 cupcake liners in muffin pan. Beat butter, gradually adding sugar, chocolate, vanilla, and Kahlua. Add 1 egg; beat. Add other egg and beat 5 minutes. Spoon filling into cupcake liners. Sprinkle almonds on each. Top with whipped topping. Chill in refrigerator for several hours. These can be frozen, thawed slightly, and served.
NOTE: Prepare two recipes to serve 24 people.

CHOCOLATE LAYER SQUARES

1 cup butter, divided
2 squares unsweetened chocolate
1 cup granulated sugar
2 eggs, beaten
    dash salt
1/4 teaspoon vanilla
1/2 cup chopped pecans
3 tablespoons milk
2 tablespoons packaged vanilla pudding mix
2 cups powdered sugar
1 4-ounce bar German sweet chocolate
1 1/2 tablespoons butter
1/2 cup flour

Melt 1/2 cup butter and unsweetened chocolate over hot water in double boiler. In mixing bowl, gradually add sugar to beaten eggs. Stir in salt, vanilla, and chocolate mixture. Fold in flour and nuts. Pour into greased 9x9x2-inch pan. Bake in 350 degree oven for 25 minutes. Cool in pan. For second layer, cream 1/2 cup butter until fluffy. Combine milk and vanilla pudding mix; add to butter and mix well. Add powdered sugar and beat until smooth. Spread over brownie layer and refrigerate until firm, about 20 minutes. For third layer, melt sweet chocolate with 1 1/2 tablespoons butter over hot water in top of double boiler. Spread over second layer. Chill again for about 10 minutes. Cut into 24 squares.

HELLO DOLLIES

1/2 cup butter
1 1/2 cups graham cracker crumbs
1 cup pecans, chopped
1 cup chocolate chips *or* butterscotch chips
1 1/3 cups flaked coconut
1 14-ounce can sweetened condensed milk

Pour melted butter into bottom of 13x9x2-inch pan. Sprinkle crumbs evenly over melted butter. Sprinkle chopped nuts evenly over crumbs. Scatter chips over nuts. Pour sweetened condensed milk evenly over coconut. Bake at 350 degrees for 25 minutes or until lightly browned. Cool 15 minutes. Cut into 24 small squares.

CHERRY SALAD

1 can sweetened condensed milk
1 9-ounce carton prepared whipped topping
1 can cherry pie filling
1 small can crushed pineapple
1 cup pecans, chopped
1 cup miniature marshmallows
1 cup coconut

Mix above ingredients and chill.
NOTE: Prepare two recipes to serve 24 people.

GLAZED FRUIT SALAD

8 20-ounce cans chunk pineapple
4 11-ounce cans mandarin orange sections, drained
4 cups maraschino cherries, drained
12 large bananas
4 cups coarsely chopped pecans
2 6-ounce packages vanilla instant pudding mix

Drain pineapple, reserving 2 cups juice. Combine fruit and pecans in a large bowl; toss gently. Combine pudding and reserved pineapple juice in a mixing bowl. Beat on high speed of electric mixer one minute. Pour pudding over fruit and pecans; toss gently.

Serves 24

FAMILY THANKSGIVING

Serves 12

Hot Cranberry Punch

24-Hour Salad

Ribbon Salad

Chicken in a Sack

Apple, Apricot, Currant, & Pecan Stuffing

Texas Potatoes

Sweet Potato Casserole in Orange Cups

French-Bean Casserole

Double Quick Dinner Rolls

Cherry Cream Cheese Pie

Pumpkin Chiffon Pie

Shopping List

1 head lettuce
3 medium onions
1 cup diced celery
2 Granny Smith or tart apples
8 large sweet potatoes
9 oranges
1 pie crust
1 graham cracker pie crust
2 cups milk
4 tablespoons unsalted butter
3 cups whipped cream
2 8-ounce packages cream cheese
2 cups + 4 tablespoons butter
1 pound Swiss cheese, grated
17 eggs
1 pound bacon
1 14 to 16 pound roasting chicken
16 ounces sour cream
16 ounces cheddar cheese, grated
1/2 pound Old English cheese, grated
1/3 cup lemon juice
1 package dry yeast

2 packages (2-pounds) hash brown potatoes
1 box raw frozen peas
2 tablespoons unflavored gelatin
1 6-ounce package lime jello
1 6-ounce package cherry jello
1 3-ounce package orange jello
1 48-ounce bottle cranberry juice cocktail
1 46-ounce can pineapple juice
1/2 cup pineapple juice
1 #2 can crushed pineapple
1 can cherry pie filling
2 16-ounce cans pumpkin
3 1/2 cups chicken broth
2 cans cream of chicken soup
4 16-ounce cans french style green beans
1/2 cup chopped pimento
2 3-ounce cans mushrooms, sliced
2 cups cheese sauce

Shopping List, continued

- 1 14-ounce can sweetened condensed milk
- 2/3 cup slivered almonds
- 1 1/3 cups crushed Ritz crackers
- 3 cups crushed cornflakes
- 1 pound (8 cups) coarsely ground bread crumbs
- 3 1/2 cups brown sugar
- 6 1/8 teaspoons salt
- 2 1/2 teaspoons pepper
- 2 3/4 cups flour
- 6 tablespoons sugar
- 2 teaspoons rubbed sage
- 1 teaspoon vanilla extract
- 1 tablespoon dried thyme
- 3 teaspoons paprika
- 3/4 teaspoon ground cloves
- 2 1/2 teaspoons ground allspice
- 2 teaspoons ginger
- 2 teaspoons pumpkin spice
- 2 1/2 teaspoons ground cinnamon
- 1/4 teaspoon ground nutmeg
- 3 teaspoons paprika
- 3/4 cup mayonnaise
- 1 3/4 cup Miracle Whip
- 1 cup peanut oil
- 1/2 cup miniature marshmallows
- 3 cups pecans
- 1 cup dried currants or raisins
- 1 cup dried apricots
- brown paper sack
- aluminum foil
- 2 tablespoons rum

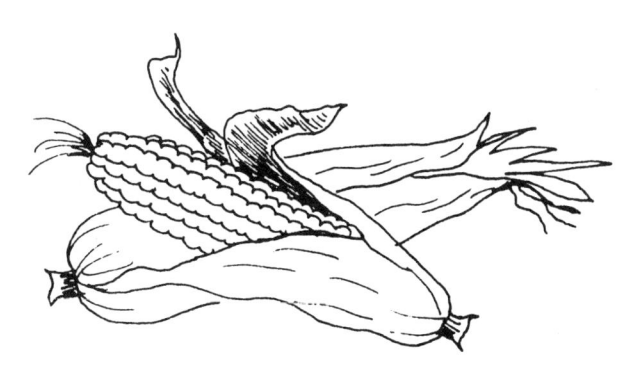

HOT CRANBERRY PUNCH

1 48-ounce bottle cranberry juice cocktail
1 cup water
1/2 cup firmly packed brown sugar
3/4 teaspoon ground cloves
1/2 teaspoon ground allspice
1/2 teaspoon ground cinnamon
1/4 teaspoon ground nutmeg
1 46-ounce can pineapple juice

Combine first 7 ingredients in a large saucepan; mix well. Bring to a boil, stirring occasionally. Add pineapple juice; return to a boil. Reduce heat and simmer the punch 5 minutes. Serve hot. Has a wonderful aroma!

Makes 3 quarts

24-HOUR SALAD

1 head lettuce, chopped fine
5 eggs
salt to taste
1 pound bacon
1 medium onion
1 box raw frozen peas
3/4 cup Miracle Whip
3/4 cup mayonnaise
1 pound Swiss cheese, grated

Using a 9x14" pan, layer finely chopped lettuce. Cook 5 eggs hard boiled. Slice and put over lettuce layer. Salt to taste. Cook 1 pound bacon; crumble on top. Slice one medium onion and put on top. Spread 1 box raw frozen peas on top. Blend Miracle Whip and mayonnaise and spread on top. Sprinkle Swiss cheese on top. Cover with foil and let stand in refrigerator for 24 hours before serving.

Serves 12

RIBBON SALAD

Poor directions

1 6-ounce package lime jello
1 6-ounce package cherry jello
1 3-ounce package orange jello
1/2 cup miniature marshmallows
1/2 cup pineapple juice
1 20-ounce can crushed pineapple
1 8-ounce package cream cheese
1 cup pecans, chopped
1 cup whipped cream
1 cup Miracle Whip

pour into your mold/dish your using –

Dissolve lime jello in 2 cups hot water. Add 2 cups cold water and refrigerate. Dissolve orange jello in 1 cup hot water, adding to it marshmallows, pineapple juice, crushed pineapple, softened cream cheese, and nuts. Chill. When orange jello mixture is partially jelled, pour on top of lime jello layer. Prepare cherry jello by dissolving jello in 2 cups hot water and stirring in two cups cold water. When orange jello mixture has jelled, pour cherry jello mixture on top of it. Refrigerate until firm.

What size dish?
Wheres the miracle whip?
+ cream added

Serves 12

CHICKEN IN A SACK

1 14 to 16 pound roasting chicken
1 teaspoon pepper
2 teaspoons salt
3 teaspoons paprika
4 teaspoons hot water
1 cup peanut oil

Combine pepper, salt, paprika, and hot water. Then add peanut oil. Rub inside and outside of chicken with oil mixture. Pour remaining oil mixture into sack. Place chicken in brown paper sack. Fold over end of sack and staple closed. Bake in a 325 degree oven approximately 20 minutes per pound. Since sack is airtight, chicken is cooked by live steam. Open sack with care.

Serves 12

APPLE, APRICOT, CURRANT, & PECAN STUFFING

- 3 1/2 cups defatted chicken broth
- 1 cup dried apricots, coarsely chopped
- 4 tablespoons unsalted butter or margarine
- 1 cup diced yellow onion
- 1 cup diced celery
- 2 Granny Smith or other tart apples, cored and cut in 1/2" cubes
- 1 tablespoon dried thyme
- 2 teaspoons rubbed sage (fresh if possible)
- 1 teaspoon freshly ground black pepper
- 1 pound (about 8 cups) coarsely ground bread crumbs for stuffing
- 2 cups shelled pecans
- 1 cup dried currants *or* raisins

Bring broth to a boil. Add apricots; remove from heat and let sit to plump for 15 minutes. Heat butter or margarine in a large pan. Add diced onion and celery; cook, covered, over low heat for 10 minutes, stirring occasionally. Add broth, apricots, apple cubes, thyme, sage, and pepper. Stir. Transfer to a large bowl. Gradually add bread crumbs, folding in gently until the stuffing is moist but not sticky. Mix in the pecans and currants. Let cool completely to room temperature before stuffing turkey *or* place dressing in a greased covered casserole, and bake in a 350 degree oven for 25 minutes. *Makes 12 cups*

TEXAS POTATOES

- 2 2-pound packages hash brown potatoes
- 16 ounces sour cream
- 16 ounces cheddar cheese, grated
- 2 teaspoons salt
- 1/2 teaspoon pepper
- 2 cans cream of chicken soup
- 1 cup chopped onion
- 1 cup butter
- 3 cups crushed cornflakes

Place frozen hash browns in bottom of buttered three-quart casserole. Break them into small pieces and mix thoroughly with sour cream, cheese, undiluted soup, onions, salt, and pepper. Melt butter in skillet and add crushed cornflakes; stir until lightly browned. Spread over casserole. Bake uncovered at 350 degrees for 30 minutes, or until bubbling around edges. *Serves 12*

SWEET POTATO CASSEROLE IN ORANGE CUPS

8 large sweet potatoes, cooked and peeled
1 cup butter, softened
juice of 3 oranges
grated rind of 2 oranges
5 eggs
1 cup brown sugar
12 orange cups (oranges halved and pulp removed)

Beat sweet potatoes with electric mixer until fluffy. Add butter, orange juice, orange rind, eggs, and sugar; beat well. Spoon potato mixture into a 3-quart casserole or orange cups. To prepare orange cups, half oranges (use the juice in the potatoes); remove pulp. Fill orange cups with potato mixture. Bake at 350 degrees for 30 minutes.

Serves 12

FRENCH BEAN CASSEROLE

4 16-ounce cans french-style green beans, drained
1/2 cup chopped pimento, drained
2 3-ounce cans mushrooms, sliced and drained
2 cups cheese sauce
2/3 cup slivered almonds
1 1/3 cups crushed Ritz crackers

Cheese Sauce:
4 tablespoons butter
4 tablespoons flour
2 cups milk
1/2 pound Old English cheese, grated

Spread green beans in bottom of 9x13-inch casserole dish. Sprinkle pimentos and mushrooms over beans and cover with cheese sauce. Sprinkle almonds on top. Bake at 350 degrees for 20 minutes. Cover with Ritz crackers and continue baking for 10 minutes.
Cheese Sauce: Melt butter; add flour, mixing well. Add milk and cook on medium heat until sauce begins to thicken. Add grated cheese. Stir sauce, cooking until cheese is melted.

Serves 12

DOUBLE QUICK DINNER ROLLS

1 package dry yeast
1 cup warm water
2 tablespoons sugar
1 teaspoon salt

1 egg
2 tablespoons butter
2 1/2 cups flour

Dissolve yeast in warm water in large bowl. Add sugar, salt, egg, butter, and 1 cup flour. Beat until smooth. Stir in remaining flour. Continue stirring until smooth. Scrape batter from sides of bowl. Cover and let rise in warm place until double (about 30 minutes). Spoon into 12 large greased muffin cups, filling each about 1/2 full. Let rise until batter reaches top of cups (20 to 30 minutes). Heat oven to 400 degrees and bake for 15 minutes. *Makes 1 dozen rolls*

CHERRY CREAM CHEESE PIE

1 graham cracker pie crust
1 14-ounce can sweetened condensed milk
1 8-ounce package cream cheese
1/3 cup lemon juice, fresh or bottled (not lemon extract)
1 teaspoon vanilla extract

Topping:
1 can cherry pie filling

Let cream cheese stand at room temperature until softened. In a medium size mixing bowl, beat cream cheese until light and fluffy. Beat in sweetened condensed milk. Add lemon juice and vanilla and stir until well mixed. Pour filling into crust. Chill until firm, about 3 hours. Top with desired amount of cherry pie filling.

Serves 6

PUMPKIN CHIFFON PIE

- 2 baked pie crusts
- 2 tablespoons unflavored gelatin
- 2 16-ounce cans pumpkin
- 2 cups brown sugar
- 6 eggs
- 2 cups whipping cream
- 2 teaspoons powdered cinnamon
- 2 teaspoons ginger
- 2 teaspoons allspice
- 2 teaspoons pumpkin spice
- 1 teaspoon salt
- 4 tablespoons granulated sugar
- 2 tablespoons rum

Bake two 9-inch pastry shells. Blend canned pumpkin, firmly packed brown sugar, slightly beaten egg yolks, powdered cinnamon, ginger, allspice, pumpkin spice, and salt. Cook this mixture in a double boiler, over boiling water, stirring constantly, until thick. Add unflavored gelatin softened in one cup cold water and stir until it is dissolved. Cool. Beat the whites of 6 eggs until they have become frothy. Add 4 tablespoons granulated sugar. Continue beating until egg whites are stiff. Fold into the cooled pumpkin mixture. Add rum and pour into the baked pie shells. Chill. Serve with whipped cream.

Serves 12

CAROLING PARTY

Serves 24

Spiced Orange Ginger Tea
Hot Dogs in Sweet and Sour Sauce
English Pea Salad
Wild Rice and Ham Chowder
Cornmeal Carrot Biscuits
Hot Punch
Oatmeal Chocolate Chip Cookies

Shopping List

- 1 12-ounce can frozen orange juice
- 8 cups cranberry juice cocktail
- 6 cups orange juice
- 1/2 cup lemon juice
- 1 cup instant tea
- 6 cups white flour
- 2 1/2 cups old fashioned oatmeal
- 1 1/2 cups cornmeal
- 3 1/2 cups white sugar
- 1 cup brown sugar
- 4 teaspoons salt
- 1/4 teaspoon pepper
- 2 tablespoons + 1 teaspoon baking powder
- 1 teaspoon baking soda
- 1 teaspoon vanilla
- 1 1/2 teaspoons thyme leaves
- 1 1/2 teaspoons nutmeg
- 2 teaspoons allspice
- 6 cinnamon sticks
- 8 whole cloves
- 3 bay leaves
- 6 slices gingerroot
- 1 cup currants or raisins
- 3 17-ounce cans whole kernel corn
- 2 16-ounce cans English peas
- 2 1/4 cups wild rice
- 3 8-ounce jars red currant jelly
- 3 tablespoons mayonnaise
- 3 tablespoons salad mustard
- 1 1/2 cups diced sweet pickle
- 3 tablespoons chopped pimento
- 12 chicken-flavored bouillon cubes *or* 1/4 cup chicken-flavored instant bouillon
- 3 pounds cubed cooked ham
- 18 hot dogs *or* 36 tiny cocktail sausages
- 3 cups cubed cheddar cheese
- 2 1/4 cups chopped pecans
- 12 ounces chocolate chips
- 1 4-ounce bar Hershey candy, grated
- 1 box garlic toast rounds
- 1 box your favorite crackers
- 1 head lettuce

Shopping List, continued

6 medium Irish potatoes
2 1/2 cups carrots
1 1/2 cups diced celery
3 cups diced onion
9 cloves garlic
1/3 cup fresh parsley

2/3 cup milk
6 cups half-and-half milk
3 cups margarine
10 eggs
1 box cocktail toothpicks

SPICED ORANGE GINGER TEA

6 quarts (24 cups) water
1 12-ounce can frozen orange juice concentrate, thawed
1 cup instant tea
1 cup sugar
6 slices gingerroot
4 cinnamon sticks
2 teaspoons whole allspice

In large saucepan, combine all ingredients; mix well. Bring to a boil; reduce heat. Simmer 10 to 20 minutes. Remove gingerroot, cinnamon sticks and allspice. Serve hot in mugs or cups. Garnish with orange slices if desired.

Makes 24 servings

HOT DOGS IN SWEET AND SOUR SAUCE

3 8-ounce jars red currant jelly
3 heaping tablespoons salad mustard
18 hot dogs sliced *or* tiny cocktail sausages

Melt jelly with mustard over low heat and blend. Add sliced hot dogs and heat. Serve warm. May be served with garlic rounds or crackers.

Makes 24 servings

ENGLISH PEA SALAD

3 16-ounce cans English peas
1 1/2 cups diced sweet pickle
3/4 cup chopped pecans
3 cups cubed cheddar cheese
1 1/2 cups diced celery
1 1/2 cups diced onions
6 hard boiled eggs
3 teaspoons salt
3 tablespoons chopped pimento
3 tablespoons mayonnaise

Chill and drain peas. Combine ingredients and toss to mix. Serve on lettuce.

Makes 24 servings

WILD RICE AND HAM CHOWDER

4 1/2 cups water
2 1/4 cups uncooked wild rice, rinsed
1 1/2 cups white flour
1 1/2 cups chopped onions
9 cloves garlic, minced
3/4 cup margarine or butter
10 cups water
12 chicken-flavored bouillon cubes *or* 1/4 cup chicken-flavored instant bouillon
4 1/2 cups cubed, peeled potatoes
1 1/2 cups chopped carrots
1 1/2 teaspoons thyme leaves
1 1/2 teaspoons nutmeg
1/4 teaspoon pepper
3 bay leaves
3 17-ounce cans whole kernel corn, undrained
6 cups half-and-half
3 pounds cubed, cooked ham
1/3 cup chopped fresh parsley

In a large saucepan, combine 4 1/2 cups water and wild rice. Bring to a boil; reduce heat. Cover; simmer 35 to 40 minutes or until rice is tender. Do not drain. Lightly spoon flour into measuring cup; level off. In large saucepan (10-quart capacity), saute onions and garlic in margarine until crisp-tender. Stir in flour. Cook 1 minute, stirring constantly. Gradually stir in 10 cups water and bouillon. Add potatoes, carrots, thyme, nutmeg, pepper, and bay leaves. Bring to a boil; reduce heat. Cover; simmer 15 to 30 minutes or until slightly thickened. Add corn. Cover; simmer an additional 15 to 20 minutes or until vegetables are tender. Stir in half-and-half, ham, and rice. Cook until thoroughly heated, stirring occasionally. Do not boil. Remove bay leaves. Garnish with parsley.

Makes 24 servings

CORNMEAL CARROT BISCUITS

2 1/2 cups white flour
1 1/2 cups cornmeal
1/2 cup sugar
2 tablespoons baking powder
1 teaspoon salt

1 1/2 cups margarine or butter
1 cup shredded carrots
1 cup currants or raisins
2/3 cup milk
2 eggs

Heat oven to 400 degrees. Lightly spoon flour into measuring cup; level off. In medium bowl, combine flour, cornmeal, sugar, baking powder, and salt; blend well. Using pastry blender or fork, cut in margarine until mixture is crumbly. Stir in carrots and currants. Add milk and egg; stir just until moistened. To form each biscuit, drop 1/4 cup of dough onto ungreased cookie sheet. Bake at 400 degrees for 10 to 12 minutes or until light golden brown. Serve warm.

Makes 24 biscuits

HOT PUNCH

8 cups cranberry juice cocktail
6 cups orange juice
1 cup sugar

1/2 cup lemon juice
8 whole cloves
2 cinnamon sticks

In large saucepan, combine all ingredients. Simmer over low heat 10 to 15 minutes or until hot, stirring occasionally. (Do not boil.) Remove cloves and cinnamon sticks. Serve hot in mugs or cups.

Makes 30 servings

OATMEAL CHOCOLATE CHIP COOKIES

- 1 cup margarine
- 1 cup sugar
- 1 cup brown sugar
- 2 eggs
- 1 teaspoon vanilla
- 2 1/2 cups old-fashioned oatmeal
- 2 cups flour
- 1 teaspoon baking powder
- 1 teaspoon baking soda
- 12 ounces chocolate chips
- 1 4-ounce bar Hershey candy, grated
- 1 1/2 cups chopped pecans

Cream margarine and sugars. Add eggs and beat well. Add vanilla. Put oatmeal, a little at a time, in blender or food processor and process to a fine powder. Combine oatmeal powder, flour, baking powder, and baking soda. Add combined dry ingredients to creamed mixture and blend well. Add chocolate chips, grated Hershey bar, and nuts to dough. Form dough into walnut-sized balls and place about 2 inches apart on ungreased cookie sheet. Bake at 375 degrees 8 minutes. Cookies should be barely brown and look a little underdone when removed from oven. They set up as they cool.

Makes 7 dozen

CHRISTMAS EVE OPEN HOUSE

Serves 50

Open House Punch
Hot Mulled Pineapple
Oriental Hot Munch
Cheese Straws
Pecan Cheese Ball
Cranberry Grape Salad
Carrot Slaw
Chicken Tetrazzini
Broccoli Balls
Cranberry Cookies
Prune Cake
Apricot Pound Cake

Shopping List

4 46-ounce cans pineapple juice
1 14-ounce can sweetened pineapple juice
46 ounces canned apricot nectar
1 14-ounce can sweetened orange-grapefruit juice
2 12-ounce cans frozen lemonade concentrate
2 cups white grape juice
1 14-ounce can tangerine juice
1/3 cup lemon juice
4 cups cranberry juice
3 8-ounce cans crushed pineapple
20 cans cream of mushroom soup
10 tablespoons soy sauce
10 teaspoons Worcestershire sauce
1 1/2 teaspoons hot sauce
2 cups fine bread crumbs
5 cups chow mein noodles
5 cups crispy rice cereal squares
5 cups crispy wheat cereal squares
5 cups broken pretzel sticks

11 1/2 cups pecan halves
2 1/2 cups cashews
2 1/2 cups chopped almonds
6 2/3 cups raisins
4 cups cooked prunes
1 cup mixed candied fruit, chopped
10 lemons
11 medium green peppers
21 medium onions
23 medium carrots
15 medium stalks celery
4 pounds fresh cranberries
3 pounds seedless grapes
20 small cloves garlic
1 quart lemon sherbet
5 chicken hens *or* 75 ounces canned chicken chunks *or* 10 pounds skinless, boned chicken breasts
41 eggs
2 3/4 cups butter
4 cups margarine
2 cups sweet milk

Shopping List, continued

4 cups buttermilk
1 1/2 pints whipping cream
5 cups sour cream
6 12-ounce cartons small curd cottage cheese
2 1/4 cups grated yellow American cheese
10 cups grated cheddar cheese
24 ounces cream cheese
5 cups grated Parmesan cheese
5 10-ounce packages spaghetti
18 10-ounce packages frozen broccoli
2 6-ounce packages apricot-flavored gelatin
4 18.5-ounce yellow cake mixes
3 cups vegetable oil
13 cups white flour
12 1/2 cups white sugar
2 3/4 cups brown sugar

9 cups powdered sugar
1 teaspoon baking powder
4 1/4 teaspoons soda
3 cups Bisquick
5 1/2 teaspoons seasoning salt
16 teaspoons salt
1 1/4 teaspoons garlic powder
1 tablespoon paprika
1 teaspoon pepper
50 whole cloves
1 teaspoon ground cloves
5 teaspoons ground nutmeg
10 teaspoons ground cinnamon
4 teaspoons allspice
1 tablespoon grated orange rind
1 cup white creme de menthe flavoring
1 teaspoon vanilla
3 pints ginger ale

OPEN HOUSE PUNCH

1 14-ounce can sweetened pineapple juice
1 14-ounce can apricot nectar
1 14-ounce can sweetened orange-grapefruit juice
2 large cans lemonade concentrate

2 cups white grape juice
1 quart lemon sherbet
1 cup white creme de menthe flavoring
3 pints dry ginger ale
1 tray tangerine juice ice cubes

Combine canned fruit juices, lemonade, and grape juice; store in a cool place. Scoop sherbet into large punch bowl; pour in mixed fruit juices and flavoring. Add ginger ale slowly. Do not blend. Add tangerine juice ice cubes.

Makes 50 servings

HOT MULLED PINEAPPLE

4 46-ounce cans pineapple juice
4 cups cranberry juice
2 cups brown sugar
2 cups granulated sugar
8 tablespoons butter, browned

4 teaspoons ground cinnamon
1 teaspoon ground nutmeg
1/2 teaspoon ground cloves
lemon slices
whole cloves

Combine first 8 ingredients. Simmer 15 minutes. Press clove into lemon slice and float in drinks.

Makes 50 servings

ORIENTAL HOT MUNCH

1/4 cup butter or margarine, melted
10 tablespoons soy sauce
10 teaspoons worcestershire sauce
1 1/2 teaspoons hot sauce
5 teaspoons seasoning salt
1 1/4 teaspoons garlic powder
5 cups chow mein noodles
5 cups crispy rice cereal squares
5 cups crispy wheat cereal squares
5 cups broken pretzel sticks
2 1/2 cups pecan halves
2 1/2 cups cashews

Combine first 6 ingredients. Combine remaining ingredients on cookie sheets. Drizzle butter mixture over cereal mixture; toss gently. Bake at 250 degrees for 1 hour, stirring occasionally. Cool and store in an airtight container.

Makes 25 cups

CHEESE STRAWS

3 cups Bisquick
1 1/8 cups sweet milk or buttermilk
3/4 cup butter
2 1/4 cups grated yellow American cheese
salt and paprika

Stir milk in Bisquick and beat vigorously for 30 seconds. Roll dough into rectangle, about 1/8-inch thick. Spread with half butter and cheese. Roll up like a jelly roll, fold ends to center, turn, and roll out again into rectangular shape. Spread with remaining butter and cheese, and repeat process. Cut into narrow strips 5 inches long. Twist. Place on baking sheet. Sprinkle with salt and paprika. Bake for 8 minutes in a 450 degree oven.

Makes 10 1/2 dozen

PECAN CHEESE BALL

24 ounces cream cheese
3 7 1/2-ounce cans crushed
   pineapple

3/4 cup chopped green pepper
6 tablespoons chopped onion
6 cups pecans

Combine cream cheese, crushed pineapple, green pepper, onion, and 3 cups of pecans. Form three cheese balls. Roll balls in remaining 3 cups pecans. Refrigerate.

Serves 50

CRANBERRY GRAPE SALAD

3 pounds cranberries, ground
3 cups sugar
3 pounds seedless grapes, halved

3 cups pecans, chopped
1 1/2 pints whipping cream,
   whipped

Mix cranberries with sugar and let set overnight in refrigerator. Mix all ingredients together and refrigerate.

Serves 50

CARROT SLAW

15 cups shredded carrots
6 2/3 cups raisins
5 cups chopped celery
5 cups sour cream
5 teaspoons salt

3 tablespoons + 1 teaspoon
   sugar
3 tablespoons + 1 teaspoon
   lemon juice
1/2 teaspoon ground cloves

Combine carrots, raisins, and celery. Mix sour cream with remaining ingredients and blend into salad. Chill.

Makes 50 servings

CHICKEN TETRAZZINI

5 hens *or* 75 ounces canned chicken chunks *or* 10 pounds skinless, boned chicken breasts
salt and pepper
5 10-ounce packages spaghetti
20 cans cream of mushroom soup
10 medium bell peppers, chopped
5 cups celery, chopped
20 small cloves garlic
20 medium onions, chopped
2 1/2 cups chopped almonds
10 cups grated cheddar cheese

If not using cooked chicken, boil hen or breasts until tender. Remove meat from bones. Cook spaghetti in chicken broth. Chop and tenderize in a little oil the celery, green pepper, onion, and garlic. Add this to spaghetti mixed with mushroom soup. Add almonds, salt, and pepper to taste. Pour into buttered casseroles. Cover with grated cheese. Bake in 350 degree oven for 30 to 40 minutes.

Serves 50

BROCCOLI BALLS

18 10-ounce packages frozen broccoli (180 ounces)
6 12-ounce cartons small curd cottage cheese (72 ounces)
5 cups grated Parmesan cheese
2 cups fine bread crumbs
3 teaspoons salt
12 eggs, beaten
2 cups white flour
1 1/2 cups butter or margarine

Cook broccoli in small amount of boiling salted water just until tender; drain and chop. Combine broccoli, cottage cheese, 2 cups Parmesan cheese, bread crumbs, salt, and eggs; stir well. Shape into 50 balls; refrigerate overnight. Roll balls in flour and place in buttered baking dishes. Dot with butter. Bake at 400 degrees for 20 minutes. Sprinkle with three cups Parmesan cheese, and bake 5 additional minutes.

Serves 50

CRANBERRY COOKIES

1/2 cup margarine, softened
1 cup sugar
3/4 cup firmly packed brown sugar
1 teaspoon vanilla extract
1/3 cup milk
1 egg
3 cups sifted all-purpose flour
1 teaspoon baking powder
1/2 teaspoon salt
1/4 teaspoon soda
2 1/2 cups fresh cranberries, coarsely chopped
1 cup mixed candied fruit, chopped
1 tablespoon grated orange rind

Combine margarine, sugar, and vanilla; cream until light and fluffy. Add milk and eggs, beating well. Combine dry ingredients; gradually add to creamed mixture, mixing well. Stir in remaining ingredients. Drop dough by tablespoonfuls onto greased cookie sheet; bake at 375 degrees for 15 to 18 minutes or until cookies are lightly browned. Place on rack to cool.

Makes about 5 dozen

PRUNE CAKE

1/2 cup margarine
1 1/2 cups sugar
3 eggs
2 cups flour
1/2 teaspoon salt
1 cup cooked prunes (save 2 tablespoons juice for frosting)
1 teaspoon soda
1 1/2 teaspoon cinnamon
1 teaspoon nutmeg
1 teaspoon allspice
1 cup buttermilk
1 cup powdered sugar (use for glaze)

Cream margarine and sugar together. Add remaining ingredients and beat with mixer. Cook in tube pan at 350 degrees for 45 minutes.
GLAZE: Blend one cup powdered sugar with two tablespoons prune juice. Drizzle over warm cake.
NOTE: Prepare FOUR recipes to serve 50 people.

APRICOT POUND CAKE

1 18 1/2-ounce yellow cake mix
1 3-ounce package apricot flavored gelatin
3/4 cup vegetable oil
4 eggs
3/4 cup apricot nectar
1 teaspoon lemon juice
GLAZE:
1 1/4 cups powdered sugar
1/4 cup apricot nectar

Combine dry cake mix and dry gelatin in medium mixing bowl. Add oil and eggs, stirring after each egg is added. Add apricot nectar and lemon juice. Mix well. Pour batter evenly into ungreased 12-cup microwave-safe fluted tube pan. Microwave on medium (50%) power for 5 minutes. Rotate cake pan. Microwave on medium for 5 to 10 more minutes. Turn the cake pan if needed for evenness of cooking. The cake is done when it is no longer doughy. Top of cake will be moist. Cool in pan on wire rack for 15 minutes. Invert onto serving platter. Pour glaze over warm cake.

GLAZE: Combine 1 to 1 1/4 cups powdered sugar and 1/4 cup apricot nectar in mixing bowl, using just enough sugar to form a thick glaze.

NOTE: Prepare FOUR recipes to serve 50 people.

CHRISTMAS DAY BRUNCH

Serves 12

Eggnog

Coffee with Cinnamon Stick

Fruit Slush Punch

Tangerine Garden Salad

Winter Spiced Pears and Apples

Do-Ahead Breakfast Souffle

Sausage Pinwheels

Grit Casserole

Apricot Nut Bread

Scrumptious Jam Cake

Poppy Seed Cake with Cream Filling and Fudge Frosting

Shopping List

2 cups buttermilk
6 1/4 cups + 1 quart milk
1/2 pint (1 cup) whipping cream
22 eggs
5 tablespoons margarine
7 1/2 cups butter
3 cans crescent rolls
3 cups diced cooked ham
1 1/2 pounds sausage
2 cups shredded cheddar cheese
2 pounds sharp cheddar cheese, grated
1 15-ounce can sweetened condensed milk
7 cups white flour
3 tablespoons cornstarch
11 cups sugar
1 1-pound package powdered sugar
4 1/4 teaspoons salt
1/2 teaspoon pepper
7 teaspoons baking powder
7 1/2 teaspoons soda
1 tablespoon garlic salt

2 bay leaves
6 teaspoons vanilla
3 tablespoons almond extract
14 cinnamon sticks
3 cloves
1 teaspoon ground cloves
3 teaspoons nutmeg
3 teaspoons cinnamon
2 teaspoons orange peel
3/4 cup poppy seed
1 1/2 cups coconut
4 squares unsweetened chocolate
3/4 cup + 2 tablespoons honey
4 cups chopped nuts
1 1/2 cups raisins
3 cups dried apricot pieces
1 1/2 cups blackberry jam
4 cups grits
2 6-ounce cans frozen orange juice concentrate
1 6-ounce can frozen lemonade concentrate
24 ounces Hawaiian punch

Shopping List, continued

24 ounces pineapple juice
1 tablespoon lemon juice
1 1-pound can coffee
4 bananas
6 medium tangerines
2 small onions
4 large ripe pears
4 large apples

12 cups mixed salad greens
3 sprigs mint
1/2 cup bottled thin French dressing
3 tablespoons Tabasco sauce
6 pitted ripe olives
2 slices white bread
2 1/2 cups red wine

EGGNOG

2 eggs, well beaten
1 15-ounce can sweetened condensed milk
1 teaspoon vanilla
1/4 teaspoon salt

1 quart homogenized milk
1/2 pint (1 cup) heavy cream, whipped
nutmeg

Combine well beaten eggs, sweetened condensed milk, vanilla, and salt until thoroughly blended. Gradually beat in milk. Gently fold in whipped cream. Pour into punch bowl or serving cups. Sprinkle with nutmeg.

Makes about 2 quarts

COFFEE WITH CINNAMON STICK

Brew desired amount of coffee. Pour coffee into cups. Use one cinnamon stick per cup of coffee.

FRUIT SLUSH PUNCH

24 ounces pineapple juice
24 ounces Hawaiian punch
1 6-ounce can frozen lemonade
1 6-ounce can frozen orange juice

4 bananas
3 cups water
1 1/2 cups sugar
1 tablespoon lemon juice

Mash bananas, adding lemon juice. Dissolve sugar in water. Add bananas and juices to sugar water. Freeze. Two hours before serving, remove from freezer. To two quarts of frozen mixture, add 16 ounces ginger ale. Stir until punch is slushy.

Serves 12

TANGERINE GARDEN SALAD

6 medium tangerines, peeled and sectioned
2 small onions, peeled, sliced, and separated into rings
1/2 cup bottled thin French dressing
4 tablespoons honey
12 cups broken mixed salad greens
6 pitted ripe olives, slivered

Place tangerine sections and onion in separate small bowls. Drizzle each with French dressing and honey; toss lightly to mix, continuing to keep tangerines and onions in their separate bowls. Chill. When ready to serve, place greens in a large salad bowl. Arrange tangerine sections in a rosette on top; place onion rings around edge; pile olive slivers in center. Drizzle with any remaining dressing in bowls.

Serves 12

WINTER SPICED PEARS AND APPLES

4 large ripe pears (Anjou are best)
4 large tart apples (Granny Smith or similar)
2 1/2 cups red wine (soft and fruity)
2 1/2 cups water
3/4 cup honey
3 teaspoons almond extract
2 bay leaves
3 cloves
2 1/2 teaspoons nutmeg
2 cinnamon sticks
3 mint sprigs

Slice pears in half, peel and remove core. Slice apples in quarters, peel and remove core. Combine wine, water, honey, almond extract, bay leaves, cloves, nutmeg, and cinnamon in a shallow saucepan or Dutch oven. Bring to a gentle boil. Add pears and apples in one layer. Cook uncovered 45 minutes or until tender. Arrange pears in center of platter, ring with apples, spoon several tablespoons poaching liquid over fruit and garnish with mint. Can be served hot or cold.

Serves 12

DO-AHEAD BREAKFAST CASSEROLE

5 tablespoons margarine
12 slices white bread
3 cups diced, cooked ham *or* 2 pounds cooked, crumbled bacon *or* 2 pounds cooked sausage
2 cups shredded cheddar cheese
1 tablespoon salt (less with bacon)
1/2 teaspoon pepper
6 eggs
3 cups milk

Butter bread. Cube bread and combine with cooked ham, cooked bacon, or cooked sausage. Add shredded cheddar cheese, salt (less with bacon), and pepper. Beat eggs until foaming. Stir in milk. Add egg and meat mixtures together. Pour into a lightly greased 13x9x2-inch baking dish. Cover and refrigerate overnight. Bake uncovered one hour at 350 degrees or until golden brown.

Serves 10 to 12

SAUSAGE PINWHEELS

3 cans crescent rolls
1 1/2 pounds sausage, cooked

Spread crumbled sausage on roll rectangles. Roll up and slice. Place on cookie sheet and bake at 375 degrees 12 to 15 minutes.

Serves 12

GRIT CASSEROLE

4 cups grits
16 cups boiling water
2 pounds sharp cheddar cheese, grated
1/2 pound butter
6 beaten eggs
1 tablespoon garlic salt
3 teaspoons Tabasco sauce

Cook grits in boiling salted water for 15 to 20 minutes. Add cheese, butter, eggs, garlic salt, and tabasco. Bake at 400 degrees for 30 minutes or until bubbly.

Serves 12

APRICOT NUT BREAD

3 cups dried apricot pieces
4 eggs
2 cups sugar
1 cup butter
4 cups sifted flour
6 teaspoons baking powder
1/2 teaspoon soda
1 1/2 teaspoons salt
1 1/2 cups orange juice
2 teaspoons orange peel
2 cups chopped nuts

Soak apricots in water for 1/2 hour. Drain and chop. Cream sugar and butter. Beat eggs and add alternately with orange juice. Then add nuts and apricots. Pour into two lined 9x5x3-inch loaf pans. Bake 1 1/2 hours in a 350 degree oven.

Serves 12

SCRUMPTIOUS JAM CAKE

6 eggs
1 1/2 cups butter
3 cups flour
1 teaspoon cloves
1 cup raisins, ground
2 cups sugar
1 cup buttermilk
1 teaspoon baking soda
3 teaspoons cinnamon
1 cup *each* pecans, coconut, and blackberry jam

Mix all ingredients together. Bake in three 9" layer pans at 350 degrees for 25 to 30 minutes. Cool; fill and frost with Jam Filling (recipe follows).

Serves 12 if sliced thinly.

JAM FILLING

1 cup butter
1 cup buttermilk
1 cup pecans
1/2 cup blackberry jam
1/2 cup raisins, ground if desired
3 cups sugar
1 teaspoon baking soda
2 teaspoons vanilla
1/2 cup coconut

Combine ingredients in a medium saucepan; cook over medium heat, stirring often, until thick.

POPPY SEED CAKE

3/4 cup poppy seeds
3/4 cup milk
3/4 cup butter
1 1/2 cups sugar

2 cups flour
1 teaspoon baking powder
1 teaspoon vanilla
4 egg whites

Soak poppy seeds in milk 4 to 6 hours. Cream butter and sugar. Add soaked seeds and milk, mixing well. Combine flour with baking powder and add to mixture. Mix in vanilla and egg whites. Bake in two layers in a 350 degree oven until wood pick inserted comes out clean. Cool on wire racks. Fill with Poppy Seed Cream Filling and ice with Chocolate Icing (recipes follow).

Serves 12 if sliced thinly

POPPY SEED CREAM FILLING

4 egg yolks
2 cups milk
1 cup sugar

3 tablespoons cornstarch
1/2 teaspoon salt

Combine ingredients until smooth. Bring to boiling and boil until thickened. Cool. Spread between layers of poppy seed cake.

CHOCOLATE FUDGE FROSTING

4 squares unsweetened chocolate
1 1-pound package powdered sugar

1/2 cup butter
1/2 cup milk
2 teaspoons vanilla

Combine chocolate and butter in small heavy saucepan. Place over low heat until melted. Remove from heat. Combine powdered sugar, milk, and vanilla in medium bowl. Stir until smooth. Add chocolate mixture. Set bowl in pan of ice and water; beat with wooden spoon until frosting is thick enough to spread and hold its shape.

CHRISTMAS DINNER

Serves 10

Hot Cinnamon Apple Punch
Crunchy Salad
Cranberry Relish Oldtime
Turkey in a Sack
Dressing
Broccoli Carrot Casserole
Party Green Beans
Sweet Potatoes with Marshmallows
Golden Potato Casserole
Dinner Rolls
Maple Pecan Pie
Snowman Cake

Shopping List

- 1 gallon apple cider
- 1 quart ginger ale
- 1/2 cup pineapple juice
- 1 1/2 cups maple-blended syrup
- 1 7-ounce can coconut
- 2 1/2 packages quick rise yeast
- 6 tablespoons ground sage
- 1/2 cup red hots
- 1 1/2 teaspoons coconut flavoring
- 3 sticks cinnamon
- 24 whole cloves
- 1/2 cup sesame seeds
- 2 3/4 teaspoons vanilla
- 1 cup sunflower seeds
- 1 cup slivered almonds
- 3 cups pecans
- 1 cup cornflakes
- 1/3 cup bread crumbs
- 1 cup quick cooking rice
- 1 16-ounce package Pepperidge Farm cornbread dressing mix
- 1 16-ounce package Pepperidge Farm herb dressing mix
- 1 can biscuits
- 1 small package miniature marshmallows
- 1 unbaked 8-inch pie shell
- 1 14- to 16-pound turkey
- 11 eggs
- 2 pints sour cream
- 1 1/2 cups margarine
- 1 cup + 5 tablespoons melted butter
- 1 cup + 3 tablespoons milk
- 3 1/4 cups (13 ounces) sharp cheddar cheese, grated
- 1/2 pound Swiss cheese, grated
- 1 cup cheddar cheese, grated
- 4 cups diced fresh broccoli *or* 2 packages chopped frozen broccoli
- 1 head iceberg lettuce
- 1 head leaf lettuce
- 1 16-ounce package cranberries
- 2 oranges
- 2 apples
- 1 lemon
- 1 bunch green onions
- 3 large onions

Shopping List, continued

- 2 bunches celery
- 8 medium potatoes
- 8 medium sweet potatoes
- 1 cup green pepper, chopped
- 2 cups shredded carrots
- 3 packages cornbread mix + ingredients as directed on package
- 2 to 4 cans chicken broth
- 4 small cans evaporated milk
- 2 cups cream of chicken soup
- 4 cans green beans
- 1 cup peanut oil
- 1 1/2 teaspoons pepper
- 7 teaspoons salt
- 1 1/2 teaspoons baking powder
- 3 teaspoons paprika
- 8 cups flour
- 1 cup brown sugar
- 4 cups powdered sugar
- 1 cup shortening
- 4 1/4 cups white sugar
- 1 grocery store paper sack

HOT CINNAMON APPLE PUNCH

1 gallon apple cider
1 quart ginger ale
1/2 cup red hot cinnamon candies
3 sticks cinnamon
24 whole cloves

In bottom of percolator, pour apple cider and ginger ale. In basket of percolator, put red hot cinnamon candies, cinnamon sticks, and whole cloves. Perk.

Makes 30 cups

CRUNCHY SALAD

1/2 cup sesame seeds
1 cup sunflower seeds
1 cup slivered almonds
1 head iceberg lettuce
1 head leaf lettuce

Preheat oven to 350 degrees. Roast sesame seeds, sunflower seeds, and almonds approximately 15 minutes or until lightly browned. Tear lettuce into bite-sized pieces and add seed mixture. Toss with a favorite Italian dressing.

Serves 10

CRANBERRY RELISH OLDTIME

1 16-ounce package raw cranberries
2 oranges, seeded and unpeeled
2 apples, cored and unpeeled
1 lemon, seeded and unpeeled
2 cups sugar
1 cup pecans, chopped (optional)

Process fruit in food processor. Add sugar and nuts. Blend and chill before serving. Keeps well in refrigerator for two weeks.

Makes 8 cups

TURKEY IN A SACK

1 teaspoon pepper
2 teaspoons salt
3 teaspoons paprika
4 teaspoons hot water
1 cup peanut oil
1 14- to 16-pound turkey (should not exceed 16 pounds)

Combine and let stand at least 10 minutes, pepper, salt, paprika, and hot water. Add peanut oil to this mixture. Wash and dry turkey; rub turkey inside and out with peanut oil mixture. Pour remaining oil mixture into large paper sack (type used in grocery store—heavy duty with no holes) and add enough peanut oil to coat inside of sack. Be sure all inner surfaces are coated with oil. Truss turkey as desired and place in sack. Fold over end of sack and staple securely. Bake in 325 degree oven approximately 20 minutes per pound. Since sack is airtight, turkey is cooked by live steam. Open sack with care.
NOTE: Do not substitute any other oil for peanut oil. Do not substitute aluminum foil for paper sack.

DRESSING

3 cooked pans of cornbread (cooled and crumbled)
1 pan biscuits (baked and crumbled)
1 16-ounce package Pepperidge Farm cornbread dressing mix
1 16-ounce package Pepperidge Farm herb dressing mix
2 large onions, chopped finely
1 bunch celery, chopped small
1 cup chopped pecans
6 tablespoons ground sage (more if desired)
2 to 4 cans chicken broth
3 eggs, well beaten
1 1/2 cups margarine, melted
1 to 2 small cans evaporated milk

Combine cornbread, biscuits, and dressings, mixing well. Cook onions and celery in water until soft, retaining broth. Mix all ingredients together using broth from onions and celery. Mixing well makes the difference in a good dressing. Place dressing in a 9x13-inch cake pan that has been sprayed with Pam. Do not cover dressing. Bake in a 350 degree oven until dressing is brown.
NOTE: Dressing may be prepared ahead of time and frozen uncooked.

BROCCOLI/CARROT CASSEROLE

2 cups shredded carrots
4 cups diced fresh broccoli *or* 2 packages chopped frozen broccoli
1 cup chopped onion
1 cup chopped celery
1 cup green pepper, chopped
1 cup quick cooking rice, uncooked
2 cups cream of chicken soup
2 small cans evaporated milk
2 teaspoons salt
1 teaspoon pepper
2 cups grated sharp cheese

Mix all ingredients in the order listed, except cheese. Bake in greased casserole, covered, at 350 degrees for 35 to 40 minutes. Remove from oven and top with cheese. Return to oven only until cheese melts.

Serves 10

PARTY GREEN BEANS

4 20-ounce cans cut or whole green beans
4 teaspoons margarine
4 teaspoons white flour
2 teaspoons salt
1/2 teaspoon pepper
2 teaspoons sugar
1 pint sour cream
1 medium onion, grated
1/2 pound Swiss cheese, grated
1 cup cheddar cheese, grated
1 cup cornflakes, crushed

Cook and drain beans. Make white sauce by melting margarine, adding flour, salt, pepper, and sugar and forming a paste. Then stir in sour cream and grated onion. Add green beans to white sauce. Place half of beans in greased 2-quart casserole, layer half of Swiss and cheddar cheese, place remaining beans on top of cheese, and layer other half of cheeses on top of beans. Then sprinkle crushed cornflakes on top of cheese. Bake 30 minutes at 350 degrees.

Serves 10 - 12

SWEET POTATOES WITH MARSHMALLOWS

8 medium large sweet potatoes
1/2 cup brown sugar
1/2 cup melted margarine
1/2 cup pineapple juice
miniature marshmallows

Pare and cut sweet potatoes into large cubes. Cover with water in 3-quart pan and cook until tender. Drain and put into large mixing bowl. Add brown sugar, margarine, and pineapple juice. Mix well with electric mixer. Continue to mix to a smooth consistency and season to taste. Pour into buttered casserole dish. Bake 30 minutes at 350 degrees. Add marshmallows to top of casserole and brown until golden.
NOTE: Two large cans of candied yams, drained, may be substituted for fresh sweet potatoes.

Serves 10

GOLDEN POTATO CASSEROLE

8 medium potatoes
1 pint sour cream
10 ounces sharp cheddar cheese, grated
1 bunch green onions, chopped
3 tablespoons milk
1 teaspoon salt
1/8 teaspoon pepper
2 tablespoons melted butter
1/3 cup bread crumbs

Scrub potatoes and cook in boiling, salted water until tender. Remove from water and cool. Peel potatoes and grate with a coarse grater. Add sour cream, cheese, onions, milk, salt, and pepper. Mix thoroughly. Turn into buttered 9x13-inch pan. Smooth with spatula. Combine melted butter and bread crumbs. Sprinkle over top. Bake in 300 degree oven for 30 minutes or until piping hot. Cut into squares and serve.

Serves 10

DINNER ROLLS

1 cup boiling water
1 cup butter
2/3 cup sugar
2 1/2 packages quick rise yeast

1 cup warm water
2 eggs
6 cups flour

Melt butter and sugar in 1 cup boiling water and let cool. Add yeast to 1 cup warm water and dissolve. Beat eggs. Mix all ingredients together, adding six cups of flour. Keep covered in refrigerator overnight. Knead, pinch off, and make into rolls, and let rise 1 hour. Bake at 325-350 degrees until browned. Muffin tins or cookie sheets may be used.

Serves 10

MAPLE PECAN PIE

1 1/2 cups maple-blended syrup
  or maple-honey flavored syrup
1 cup coarsely chopped pecans
1 unbaked 8-inch pie shell
3 tablespoons butter

1/4 cup sugar
2 tablespoons all purpose flour
1/4 teaspoon salt
3 eggs, well beaten
1/2 teaspoon vanilla

Pour syrup into 1 1/2-quart saucepan; boil gently, uncovered for 8 minutes. Cool about 15 minutes. Sprinkle nuts in pie shell. Cream butter; blend in sugar, flour, and salt. Add eggs, syrup, and vanilla; mix well. Pour into shell. Bake at 375 degrees for 40 to 45 minutes or until pie is completely puffed across top and browned. Cool. Serve plain or top with prepared whipped topping or whipping cream if desired.

SNOWMAN CAKE

3/4 cup margarine
1 cup sugar
1/2 cup brown sugar
1 teaspoon vanilla
1/2 teaspoon coconut flavoring
3 eggs

1 1/2 cups all-purpose flour
1 1/2 teaspoons baking powder
1/2 teaspoon salt
3/4 cup milk
1 7-ounce can coconut

Cream the first five ingredients well. Add eggs; beat well. Combine dry ingredients; add to creamed mixture alternately with milk, ending with milk. Grease a 1 1/2-quart ovenproof mixing bowl, two three-cup ovenproof mixing bowls, and one 5-ounce ovenproof custard cup. Measure 2 cups batter into large bowl. Measure 1 cup batter into two medium bowls. Fill custard cup half full with batter. (Divide any remaining batter between larger bowls.) Bake at 350 degrees for 50 to 55 minutes for large and medium bowls; 20 to 25 minutes for custard cup. Cool in bowls 10 minutes; turn out onto wire racks and cool completely.

Frosting:

4 cups powdered sugar
5 tablespoons margarine
1 1/4 teaspoons vanilla

1/2 teaspoon coconut flavoring
1/2 teaspoon salt
1/4 cup milk

Cream 1 cup powdered sugar and next four ingredients. Add milk alternately with remaining powdered sugar. Mix until creamy and smooth. Add more sugar or more milk, if necessary, to make a good spreading consistency.

Before frosting cooled cake, trim top of largest cake if necessary to level. To keep plate clean, arrange four strips of waxed paper around edge of plate. (Remove after frosting and decorating.) Put largest cake on serving plate, rounded side up. Spread with frosting. Spread a small amount of frosting on flat sides of medium-sized cakes; put frosted sides together to form a ball. Center the ball on the largest cake. Secure with toothpicks if necessary. Frost all sides. Place smallest cake on top of ball to form the head. Secure with toothpicks if necessary and frost. Gently pat coconut over entire snowman. Decorate with candies; gumdrops for eyes and buttons, licorice ropes for scarf and mouth, candy canes for arms. Make top hat from black construction paper.

Serves 10

LET'S GET RID OF
THE TURKEY DINNER

Serves 6

Snowball Salad
Goodbye Turkey Casserole
Dilly Cheese Bread
Eloquent Dessert of Blueberries

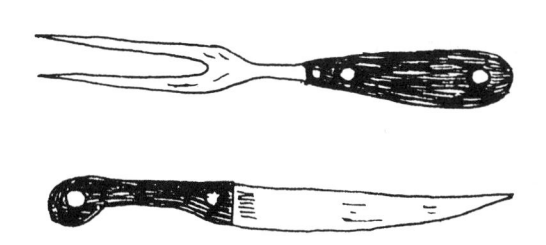

Shopping List

- 1 2-layer size package yellow cake mix
- 1 cup sugar
- 4 cups + 5 tablespoons white flour
- 1 teaspoon salt
- 1/4 teaspoon onion salt
- 1 tablespoon dill seed
- 1/2 pound marshmallows (small or large)
- 2 packages dry yeast
- 1 7-ounce can crushed pineapple
- 1/4 cup maraschino cherries, chopped
- 1 can blueberry pie filling
- 2 tablespoons lemon juice
- 1 1/2 cups turkey or chicken broth
- 1 1/2 cups canned asparagus
- 1 cup chopped pecans
- 2 tablespoons slivered almonds
- 2 bananas
- 3 cups milk
- 1/2 cup sour cream
- 1/2 pint whipping cream
- 1/2 cup margarine
- 1/4 cup butter
- 2 eggs
- 2 cups cooked turkey
- 1/2 cup grated American cheese
- 1 cup (4 ounces) shredded Swiss cheese
- 1/2 cup grated Parmesan cheese
- 1 8-ounce carton whipped topping
- 1 1/3 cups minute rice
- 1 cup grapenuts dry cereal
- 20 graham crackers
- aluminum foil

SNOWBALL SALAD

3/4 cup sugar
1/2 cup sour cream
1 8-ounce carton prepared whipped topping
1 tablespoon lemon juice

2 bananas
1/2 cup chopped pecans
1 7-ounce can crushed pineapple
1/4 cup maraschino cherries, chopped

Mix sugar, sour cream, and lemon juice until sugar is dissolved. Fold in prepared whipped topping, mashed bananas, pecans, drained pineapple, and chopped maraschino cherries. Refrigerate.

Serves 6

GOODBYE TURKEY CASSEROLE

5 tablespoons flour
1 teaspoon salt
1/4 teaspoon onion salt
1/4 cup melted butter
2 1/2 cups milk or light cream
1 1/3 cups minute rice
1 1/2 cups turkey or chicken broth

1/2 cup grated American cheese
1 1/2 cups cooked asparagus
2 cups turkey
2 tablespoons toasted slivered almonds

Mix flour, half of salt, and onion salt in bowl. Melt butter in top of double boiler. Stir flour mixture into butter, gradually stirring in milk. Stir occasionally until thickened. Pour minute rice into 2-quart shallow baking dish. Combine broth and remaining salt and pour over rice. Sprinkle half of cheese over rice. Top with asparagus; then add turkey. Pour on sauce. Sprinkle with remaining cheese. Bake at 375 degrees about 20 minutes. Top with almonds.
NOTE: You may substitute chicken for turkey and broccoli for asparagus.

Serves 6

DILLY CHEESE BREAD

- 2 packages active dry yeast
- 2 cups warm water (115 to 120 degrees)
- 2 eggs
- 1 package two-layer size yellow cake mix
- 1 cup grape nuts
- 1 cup shredded Swiss cheese (4 ounces)
- 1/2 cup Parmesan cheese
- 1 tablespoon dill seed
- 4 cups all purpose flour

In mixing bowl, dissolve yeast in warm water. Add eggs, beating until blended. Add dry cake mix, cereal, Swiss cheese, Parmesan, and dill seed. Beat well. Stir in flour. Divide batter between two well-greased 8x4x2 loaf pans. Cover and let rise in warm place 1 to 1 1/2 hours or until nearly doubled. Bake in 350 degree oven for 55 to 60 minutes or till bread sounds hollow when lightly tapped. Cover with foil the last 15 minutes to prevent over-browning. Loosen edges with metal spatula; remove to cooling rack. Makes two loaves. Recipe may be halved.

Serves 6 - 12

ELOQUENT DESSERT OF BLUEBERRIES

- 20 graham crackers, crushed
- 1 stick margarine
- 1/2 cup chopped pecans
- 2 tablespoons sugar
- 1/2 pound marshmallows
- 1/2 cup milk
- 1/2 pint whipped cream
- 1 can blueberry pie filling
- 1 tablespoon lemon juice

Make a graham cracker crust using crushed graham crackers, margarine, chopped pecans, and sugar. Spread one-half crust mixture into greased 6x10 pan. In a saucepan, melt marshmallows in milk. Cool at room temperature. Add 1/2 whipped cream. Spread one-half marshmallow mixture over crumbs. Spread blueberry pie filling mixed with lemon juice over marshmallow mixture. Add remaining marshmallow mixture and top with remaining mixture of crackers. Chill overnight.

Serves 6

SUBSTITUTE RECIPES

Beverages — 129

Strawberry Crush

Mint Julep

Almond Tea

Lemonade with Frozen Tea Cubes

Appetizers — 131

Broiled Grapefruit

Salmon Party Rolls with Crackers

Ham and Cheese Rolls with Crackers

Salads — 132

Dijon Potato Salad

Classic Waldorf Salad

Fresh Fruit Shell Salad

Chicken Fruit Salad

with Fruit Whipped Dressing

Watergate Salad

Bing Cherry Salad and Dressing

Wilted Lettuce

Minted Fruit Bowl

Orange Souffle Mold

Main Dishes — 136

Black Bean Soup

Easy Day Stew

Split Pea Soup

Peanut Butter Soup

Salmon Loaf

Southern Shrimp and Chicken

Ground Beef Special

Beef Stroganoff

Meatloaf Supreme

Lasagna

Sukiyaki

Ham Loaf

Nutty Baked Chicken

Chicken and Dressing Casserole

Spicy Chicken with Peanuts

Herbed Chicken

Veal Parmigiana

Coffee Flavored Pot Roast

Vegetables — *146*

Celery Almandine

Yellow Squash

Baked Acorn Squash

Green Chili Souffle

Green Chili Hominy

Spinach Souffle Baked in Squash

Black-Eyed Pea Stew

Breads — *149*

90-Minute Pecan Cornbread

Apricot Nut Bread

Melt-in-your-Mouth Biscuits

Perfect Popovers

Mini-Morsel Muffins

Sour Cream Pancakes

Swedish Pancakes

Ebelskievers

Desserts — 153

Peanut Butter Balls

Toll House Cookie Brittle

Ranger Cookies

Winter Fruit Splendor

Apple Crisp

Bananas Barron

Peaches or Pears Cardinale

Holiday Cranberry Cake

Peaches and Cream Cake

Fresh Apple Cake

Cheese Cake

Orange-Pecan Pie

French Strawberry Pie

Strawberry Pie

Key Lime Macadamia Dream Pie

French Silk Pie

Beverages

STRAWBERRY CRUSH

1 1/2 cups fresh strawberries
1 1/2 cups orange juice
3 tablespoons sugar
1 1/2 cups crushed ice

Put everything in blender. Cover and blend for 10 seconds. Serve cold.

Serves 4

MINT JULEP

2 1/2 cups water
2 cups sugar
  juice of 2 oranges
juice of 2 lemons
crushed mint

Boil water and sugar 10 minutes. Add remaining ingredients. Cover with tight lid and cool. Serve over ice.

Serves 4 to 6

ALMOND TEA

3 small tea bags
2 cups boiling water
3/4 cup sugar
4 cups water
10 tablespoons real lemon juice
2 teaspoons almond extract
1 teaspoon vanilla extract

Steep tea bags in 2 cups boiling water for 10 minutes. Boil sugar in 4 cups of water for 5 minutes. Combine lemon juice, almond extract, and vanilla extract. Combine tea and sugar mixtures with lemon juice and flavorings. Serve over ice.

Serves 6

LEMONADE WITH FROZEN TEA CUBES

juice of 4 medium lemons (about 3/4 cup)
1/2 cup sugar
2 cups cold water
frozen tea cubes (recipe follows)
lemon slices, optional

Combine lemon juice, sugar, and water, stirring until sugar dissolves. To serve, place several frozen tea cubes in each glass. Garnish with lemon slices if desired.

Serves 4

Frozen Tea Cubes
1 1/2 cups water
10 whole cloves
2 2-inch cinnamon sticks
4 regular tea bags
1 1/2 cups cold water

Combine 1 1/2 cups water, cloves, and cinnamon sticks in a saucepan; bring to a boil. Reduce heat, simmer 5 minutes; remove from heat. Pour over tea bags; cover and let stand 10 minutes. Discard tea bags and spices; add 1 1/2 cups cold water to tea mixture. Pour tea into ice cube trays and freeze.

Makes 2 dozen cubes

Appetizers

BROILED GRAPEFRUIT

1/2 grapefruit	1/4 teaspoon butter
2 tablespoons Kirsch	

Using grapefruit knife, separate sections and remove visible seeds. Pour 2 tablespoons Kirsch over each half. Dot with butter. Broil until butter is melted and slightly browned.

Serves 2

SALMON PARTY ROLL

1 1-pound can salmon	1 teaspoon prepared horseradish
1 8-ounce package cream cheese, softened	1/4 teaspoon salt
	1/4 teaspoon liquid smoke
1 tablespoon lemon juice	1/2 cup chopped pecans
2 teaspoons grated onion	3 tablespoons snipped parsley

Drain and flake salmon, removing skin and bones. Combine salmon with next 6 ingredients; mix thoroughly. Chill several hours. Combine pecans and parsley. Shape salmon mixture in an 8x2-inch roll; roll in nut mixture. Chill well. Serve with crackers.

Serves 8

HAM AND CHEESE ROLLS

1 package Danish ham slices, 6 slices	1/2 cup green onions, chopped fine
1 8-ounce package cream cheese	1 tablespoon mayonnaise or milk

Mix cream cheese with enough milk or mayonnaise to soften. Mix in chopped green onions. Spread on ham slices and make into a roll. Refrigerate. Slice and serve on crackers.

Serves 8

Salads
DIJON POTATO SALAD

1 cup real or light mayonnaise
2 tablespoons dijon mustard
2 tablespoons chopped fresh dill
 or 1 1/2 teaspoon dried dillweed
1 teaspoon salt
1/4 teaspoon pepper
1 1/2 pounds small red potatoes, cooked and quartered
1 cup sliced radishes
1/2 cup chopped green onions

Combine mayonnaise, mustard, dill, salt, and pepper. Combine potatoes, radishes, and green onions. Combine the two mixtures and refrigerate for several hours before serving. *Serves 6 to 8*

CLASSIC WALDORF SALAD

1/2 cup real or light mayonnaise
1 tablespoon sugar
1 tablespoon lemon juice
1/8 teaspoon salt
3 medium apples, diced
1 cup sliced celery
1/2 cup chopped walnuts

Combine first 4 ingredients. Stir in remaining ingredients. Cover; chill. *Makes 5 1/2 cups*

FRESH FRUIT SHELL SALAD

1/2 of a 1-pound package medium shell macaroni
1 8-ounce container plain lowfat yogurt
1/4 cup frozen orange juice, thawed
1 15-ounce can pineapple chunks, drained
1 large orange, peeled, sectioned, and seeded
1 cup seedless red grapes, cut in halves
1 cup seedless green grapes, cut in halves
1 apple, cored and chopped
1 banana, sliced

Prepare macaroni as package directs; drain. In small bowl, blend yogurt and orange juice concentrate. In large bowl, combine remaining ingredients including macaroni. Add yogurt mixture; toss to coat. Cover; chill thoroughly. Toss gently before serving. *Serves 10*

CHICKEN FRUIT SALAD

1 16-ounce can pineapple chunks
1 apple
3 cups cooked, diced chicken
1 cup seedless grapes
Fruit-Whipped Cream Dressing (recipe follows)
lettuce cups
1/2 cup toasted, slivered almonds

Drain pineapple chunks, reserving juice. Core and slice apple, dipping slices into pineapple juice. Combine pineapple, apple, chicken, and grapes; chill until serving time. Add Fruit-Whipped Cream dressing and toss lightly. Serve on lettuce cups and top with almonds.

Fruit-Whipped Cream Dressing
3 tablespoons butter or margarine
3 tablespoons flour
1/4 cup sugar
1 teaspoon salt
1/3 cup lemon juice
1/3 cup pineapple juice
2 egg yolks
1/2 cup whipping cream

Melt butter or margarine and stir in flour until smooth. Add sugar, salt, and fruit juices. Cook until thickened, stirring constantly. Beat egg yolks slightly and stir in hot mixture. Cook about 2 minutes; chill. Whip cream and fold into chilled dressing.

WATERGATE SALAD

1 3-ounce package instant pistachio pudding
1 12-ounce carton prepared whipped topping
1 cup miniature marshmallows
1/2 cup pecans, chopped
1 15-ounce can drained crushed pineapple

Drain pineapple juice into a large bowl; stir in pudding mix. Fold in remaining ingredients. Chill.

Serves 8

BING CHERRY SALAD

1 No. 2 can pitted bing cherries	2 cups fruit juice
1 cup crushed pineapple	2 6 1/2 ounce bottles Coca-cola
2 3-ounce packages cherry gelatin	1 cup chopped California walnuts or pecans

Drain juice from cherries and pineapple. Reserve three cups fruit juice. (One cup pineapple juice is needed for dressing.) Bring two cups juice to boiling and pour over gelatin, stirring until completely dissolved. When cool, add Coca-cola; stir and chill in refrigerator until partly congealed. Add drained cherries, pineapple, and nuts and pour into mold that has been rinsed in cold water. When firm, unmold on salad greens and serve with the following dressing:

2 eggs	1 tablespoon flour
1 cup pineapple juice	1 tablespoon butter
1 lemon	1/2 cup whipped cream *or* 1/2 cup Miracle Whip salad dressing
1/2 cup sugar	

Mix flour, salt, and sugar. Add lemon and pineapple juices and beaten eggs. Cook until mixture coats a spoon. Remove mixture from heat and add butter. Cook until thick. Cool. Add 1/2 cup whipped cream *or* salad dressing.

Serves 8

WILTED LETTUCE

4 slices bacon, chopped	2 tablespoons chopped chives
1/4 cup Good Season's French dressing	2 tablespoons vinegar
	1 tablespoon sugar
1/4 teaspoon celery salt	2 medium heads leaf lettuce

Tear lettuce leaves into bite-size pieces and place in a bowl. Saute bacon in pan until brown and crisp. Add dressing; keep over heat. Add celery salt, chives, vinegar, and sugar. Stir mixture well, bringing to a boil. Pour mixture over lettuce in bowl, cover with plate and allow to steam for 5 to 6 minutes. Remove cover, toss lettuce, and serve on warmed plate.

Serves 4

MINTED FRUIT BOWL

1/2 cup sugar
1/2 cup water
1/2 cup firmly packed mint leaves
1 small ripe pineapple, cubed
1 pint strawberries, halved
1/2 honeydew melon, cubed
3 tablespoons fresh lemon juice
2 tablespoons bourbon or rum

Combine sugar, water, and 1/2 cup mint in saucepan. Boil, stirring constantly, until sugar dissolves, about one minute. Strain syrup into bowl. Add remaining ingredients; toss.

Serves 8

ORANGE SOUFFLE MOLD

2 envelopes unflavored gelatin
2 cups sugar
dash salt
4 egg yolks
2 1/2 cups orange juice
1 teaspoon grated orange peel
1 teaspoon grated lemon peel
3 tablespoons fresh lemon juice (about 1 lemon)
1 cup orange sections (about 3 to 4 oranges), white membrane removed, cut in half
1/2 cup heavy cream, whipped

Thoroughly mix gelatin, sugar, and salt in saucepan. Beat egg yolks and 1 cup orange juice, stir into gelatin mixture. Cook over medium heat, stirring constantly, just until mixture comes to boil. Remove from heat, stir in orange and lemon peels and remaining juices. Chill, stirring occasionally, until mixture mounds when dropped from spoon. Add whipped cream and place in individual molds. Refrigerate until set.

Serves 6 to 8

Main Dishes

BLACK BEAN SOUP

1 16-ounce package dried black beans
7 cups water
1 14 1/2-ounce can diluted chicken broth
1 small ham hock
1 tablespoon butter or margarine
2 cloves garlic, crushed
1 small hot pepper, chopped
1 medium onion, chopped
1 stalk celery, chopped
1 bay leaf
1/2 teaspoon salt
1/2 teaspoon pepper
1/2 teaspoon dry mustard
1/3 cup dry sherry
feta cheese (optional)

Sort and wash beans; place in Dutch oven. Add 7 cups water. Bring to boil; cover and cook 2 minutes. Remove from heat; let stand 1 hour. Add chicken broth and remaining ingredients except sherry and feta cheese. Bring to boil; cover, reduce heat, and simmer 2 to 2 1/2 hours, stirring occasionally. Discard bay leaf. Remove ham hock; cut off meat and dice. Discard bone, and set the meat aside. Measure 4 cups soup and pour into container of an electric blender; process until smooth. Return mixture to Dutch oven. Add diced ham and sherry. Bring mixture to boil; reduce heat, and simmer 10 minutes. Sprinkle each serving with feta cheese if desired. NOTE: Seeds in small hot pepper make soup very hot. For a milder soup, remove seeds before chopping pepper.

Serves 4 to 6

EASY DAY STEW

2 pounds beef stew, cut into pieces
3 stalks celery, cut into slices
2 small onions, cut up
4 medium potatoes, cubed
1 tablespoon sugar
1/2 tablespoon salt
2 tablespoons tapioca
pepper to taste
1 cup tomato juice

Put all ingredients into covered casserole. Bake at 250 degrees for 4 hours.

Serves 4

SPLIT PEA SOUP

1 pound dried, split green peas
8 cups water
2 ham hocks *or* 2 pieces smoked ham
1 16-ounce can tomatoes, diced
1 cup onion, chopped
1 cup celery, chopped
1/2 cup shredded carrots
2 teaspoons dried parsley
2 tablespoons vinegar
1/2 teaspoon garlic powder
2 1/2 teaspoons seasoned salt
1/2 teaspoon crushed, dried oregano
chicken broth

In a heavy pan, bring peas, water, and ham to boil; boil slowly 2 minutes. Turn off heat; cover and let stand 1 hour. Add remaining ingredients; cover pot and simmer 2 1/2 hours. If soup is too thick, thin with chicken broth.

Serves 6

PEANUT BUTTER SOUP

1 stalk celery, coarsely chopped
1 medium carrot, coarsely chopped
2 tablespoons onion, chopped
3/4 cup water
2 chicken flavored *or* beef flavored bouillon cubes
2 cups water, divided
1/2 cup creamy peanut butter
1/4 teaspoon pepper
1 tablespoon cornstarch
1/2 cup half and half
carrot strips (optional)
chopped peanuts (optional)

Combine first 4 ingredients in a saucepan; cover and cook over low heat 10 minutes or until tender. Add bouillon cubes and 1 1/2 cups water; cook, uncovered, until bouillon cubes dissolve. Pour mixture into container of electric blender, and add peanut butter and pepper; process until smooth. Return mixture to saucepan. Combine cornstarch and remaining 1/2 cup water, stirring constantly, until thoroughly heated. If desired, garnish individual servings with carrot strips and chopped peanuts.

Serves 4

SALMON LOAF

1 1-pound can salmon	2 eggs, beaten
1 cup cheese, grated	1 teaspoon salt
1/2 cup olives (green stuffed or ripe), chopped	1/4 teaspoon pepper
	2 tablespoons butter
1 cup bread crumbs	2 tablespoons parsley, chopped
3/4 cup milk	2 tablespoons onion, chopped

Flake salmon; combine with remaining ingredients. Press into greased loaf pan and bake at 350 degrees for 30 minutes. Serve hot or cold.

Serves 4 to 6

SOUTHERN SHRIMP AND CHICKEN

5 slices bacon	1 8-ounce bottle clam juice
1 1/2 pounds skinless, boneless chicken thighs, halved	1/2 teaspoon salt
	1/4 teaspoon red pepper
3 tablespoons white flour	1/4 teaspoon white pepper
1 cup chopped onions	1/4 teaspoon thyme
1 cup chopped celery	1 pound medium shrimp, peeled
1/2 cup chopped green pepper	2 tablespoons chopped fresh parsley
2 teaspoons chopped garlic	
1 14 1/2-ounce can chicken broth	

Cook bacon in skillet until crisp; drain on paper towels and crumble. Discard all but 2 tablespoons drippings and brown chicken over high heat. Transfer chicken to bowl. Add flour to pan; cook until browned. Add onions, celery, green pepper, and garlic. Cook about 5 minutes. Stir in broth, clam juice, salt, peppers, and thyme. Bring to boil, stirring constantly. Reduce heat; simmer 5 minutes. Return chicken to pan; cook 5 minutes more. Stir in shrimp and cook about 2 minutes. Sprinkle with bacon and parsley. Serve with rice.

Serves 6

GROUND BEEF SPECIAL

2 pounds ground beef
1 cup onion, chopped
2 teaspoons prepared mustard
3 teaspoons salt
1/8 teaspoon pepper

1 8-ounce can tomato sauce
1 cup tomato juice
2 tablespoons vinegar
1/4 cup sliced stuffed olives

Brown ground beef in large skillet. Add onion; cook about 5 minutes. Add remaining ingredients except olives; simmer about 20 minutes. Stir in olives. NOTE: Use for spaghetti sauce, green pepper stuffing or hot sandwiches.

Makes 1 1/2 quarts

BEEF STROGANOFF

1 tablespoon flour
1/2 teaspoon salt
1 pound beef sirloin cut in 1/4" strips
2 tablespoons butter
1 cup thinly sliced mushrooms
1/2 cup onion, chopped
1 clove garlic, minced

2 tablespoons butter
3 tablespoons flour
1 tablespoon tomato paste
1 1/4 cups beef stock *or* 1 can beef broth
1 cup sour cream
2 tablespoons cooking sherry

Combine 1 tablespoon flour and salt; dredge meat in mixture. Heat skillet; add 2 tablespoons butter. When butter is melted, add sirloin strips and brown quickly, flipping meat to turn all sides. Add mushroom slices, onion, and garlic. Cook 3 or 4 minutes or until onion is barely tender. To make sauce, remove meat and mushrooms from skillet. Add 2 tablespoons butter to pan drippings; when melted, blend in 3 tablespoons flour. Add tomato paste. Slowly pour in cold meat stock and cook, stirring constantly until mixture thickens. Return browned meat and mushrooms to skillet. Stir in sour cream and sherry; heat briefly.

Serves 2

MEATLOAF SUPREME

1 slice bread, broken into crumbs
2 beaten eggs
1/2 cup tomato juice *or* tomato sauce
2 tablespoons parsley
1/2 teaspoon oregano
1/4 teaspoon pepper
1/2 teaspoon salt

1 clove garlic, minced
2 pounds ground beef
8 slices boiled ham
1 1/2 cups mozzarella cheese, grated
3 slices mozzarella cheese
1 8-ounce can tomato sauce

Combine first 8 ingredients. Add ground meat and mix. Roll meat into a 10x12 rectangle on foil. Place boiled ham slices and grated mozzarella cheese on top, then jelly roll. Place in baking dish. Bake at 350 degrees uncovered for 1 hour and 15 minutes. Last five minutes, put 3 slices mozzarella cheese and 1 can tomato sauce on top.

Serves 8

LASAGNA

- 1 pound smoked sausage
- 1 pound ground beef
- 1/2 cup onion, finely chopped
- 2 cloves garlic, crushed
- 2 tablespoons sugar
- 1 tablespoon salt
- 1 1/2 teaspoons dried basil
- 1/2 teaspoon fennel seed
- 1/4 teaspoon pepper
- 1/4 cup chopped parsley
- 4 cups canned tomatoes, undrained
- 2 6-ounce cans tomato paste
- 1 tablespoon salt
- 12 curly lasagna noodles (3/4 of a 1-pound package)
- 1 15-ounce container ricotta *or* cottage cheese, drained
- 1 egg
- 1/2 teaspoon salt
- 3/4 pound mozzarella cheese
- 1 3-ounce jar grated Parmesan cheese (3/4 cup)

Brown sausage and beef, adding onion and garlic until well-browned. Add sugar, 1 tablespoon salt, basil, fennel, pepper, and half of parsley; mix well. Add tomatoes, tomato paste, and 1/2 cup water, mashing tomatoes with wooden spoon. Bring to boiling, reduce heat; simmer, covered and stirring occasionally until thick—1 1/2 hours. In 8-quart kettle, bring 3 quarts water and 1 tablespoon salt to boiling. Add lasagna noodles 2 or 3 at a time. Return to boiling; boil, uncovered and stirring occasionally 10 minutes or until tender. Drain and rinse with cold water. Dry lasagna noodles on paper towels. Preheat oven to 375 degrees. Combine ricotta, egg, remaining parsley, and salt; mix well. In bottom of a 13x9x2-inch baking dish, spoon 1 1/2 cups sauce. Layer with 6 lasagna noodles lengthwise and overlapping, to cover. Spread with half of ricotta cheese mixture; top with third of mozzarella. Spoon 1 1/2 cups sauce over cheese; sprinkle with Parmesan. Spread with remaining sauce; add 6 lasagna noodles; top with rest of mozzarella and Parmesan. Cover with foil, tucking around edge. Bake 25 minutes; remove foil; bake, uncovered, 25 minutes longer, or until bubbly. Cool 15 minutes before serving.

Serves 8

SUKIYAKI

1 1/2 pounds beef sirloin, 1" thick
1 beef bouillon cube
1/2 cup boiling water
1/4 cup soy sauce
1/4 cup dry sherry
2 tablespoons sugar
1/8 teaspoon pepper
2 tablespoons cooking oil
1 16-ounce can bean sprouts, drained and rinsed
1 cup green onion pieces, cut 1 1/2" long
1 cup celery pieces, cut 1 1/2" long
1 cup sliced fresh mushrooms
1 5-ounce can bamboo shoots, drained
1 5-ounce can water chestnuts, drained and sliced

Cut meat across grain in paper-thin slices. (Cutting is easier if meat is partially frozen.) Dissolve bouillon cube in boiling water; stir in soy sauce, wine, sugar, and pepper. In electric skillet or 12-inch skillet, quickly brown about 1/3 of the meat at a time in hot oil. Push meat to one side of skillet. Pour about 1/2 cup of soy mixture into skillet. Keeping in separate groups, add bean sprouts, green onions, celery, mushrooms, bamboo shoots, and water chestnuts; cook uncovered, over high heat for 1 to 2 minutes, lifting vegetables gently to stir. Pour remaining soy mixture into skillet; cook 1 minute more or until vegetables are just heated through. Serve with steamed rice.

Serves 6

HAM LOAF

1/2 cup brown sugar
1/2 cup vinegar
1 teaspoon dry mustard
1 pound fresh ham, ground
1 pound cured ham, ground
1/2 cup milk
1/2 cup cornflakes, crushed
1 egg

Mix ham, milk, cornflakes, and egg. Shape into loaf. Combine brown sugar, vinegar, and dry mustard, spreading on top of loaf. Bake 30 minutes at 350 degrees. Reduce heat to 300 degrees and bake for 45 minutes. Baste frequently with the mustard sauce.

Serves 6 to 8

NUTTY BAKED CHICKEN

4 cups cooked, cubed chicken
4 cups thinly sliced celery
1 cup chopped pecans
1 1/2 cups grated cheese

2 cups mayonnaise
4 tablespoons onion
4 tablespoons lemon juice

Lightly toss the chicken, celery, and pecans together. Puree a sauce of mayonnaise, onion, lemon juice, and 1 cup cheese in a blender. Toss the chicken mixture with the sauce. Pour into a 9x13" casserole. Top with 1/2 cup cheese and bake at 375 degrees for 15 to 20 minutes. Serve hot.

Serves 6 to 8

CHICKEN AND DRESSING CASSEROLE

1 package Pepperidge Farm herbed stuffing mix
1/2 cup melted margarine
1 cup water or chicken broth
2 1/2 cups cooked chicken, cubed
1/2 cup onion, finely chopped
1/4 cup celery, finely chopped

1/2 cup mayonnaise
3/4 teaspoon salt
2 eggs
1 1/2 cups milk
1 can cream of mushroom soup
2 cups sharp cheddar cheese, grated

Combine stuffing mix with melted margarine and 1 cup water or chicken broth. Place half of mixture in casserole. Combine cooked chicken, chopped onion, chopped celery, mayonnaise, and salt. Spread on top of mixture in casserole. Cover with remaining stuffing mix. Mix 2 eggs and 1 1/2 cups milk. Pour over top of casserole. Cover with foil and refrigerate overnight. Remove from refrigerator one hour before baking. Spread 1 can undiluted cream of mushroom soup over top. Bake uncovered at 325 degrees for 40 to 50 minutes. Sprinkle grated cheese on top and return to oven to melt cheese.

Serves 8

SPICY CHICKEN WITH PEANUTS

2 whole chicken breasts, boned, skinned and cubed
1 egg white
1 tablespoon cornstarch
2 tablespoons soy sauce
2 green onions, sliced
8 whole dried red peppers *or* 1/4 teaspoon crushed red pepper
1 teaspoon sugar
1 teaspoon cornstarch
2 tablespoons sherry
1 cup peanut oil
2 tablespoons peanut oil
1/2 cup cocktail peanuts

Combine beaten egg white, 1 teaspoon cornstarch, and 1 tablespoon soy sauce; mix well. Add chicken and refrigerate 1 hour or longer. Combine onions and dried peppers (tips removed) or red pepper, set aside. Combine sugar, 1 teaspoon cornstarch, remaining 1 tablespoon soy sauce, water, and sherry; set aside. Heat 1 cup peanut oil in wok to 275 degrees. Stir in chicken mixture. Stir-fry until chicken turns white, about 1 minute. Remove chicken to a colander and drain. Heat 2 tablespoons oil in same wok over high heat. Add onions, red pepper, and cooked chicken; stir-fry 1 minute. Add soy sauce mixture to chicken while stirring over high heat in wok until mixture is lightly glazed. Add peanuts and mix well. Serve over hot cooked rice if desired.

Serves 2

HERBED CHICKEN

6 chicken breasts, skinned and boned (uncooked)
6 slices Swiss cheese
1 can cream of chicken soup
1/2 cup milk
1/2 cup white wine *or* cooking sherry
1 package herbed dressing
1 cup margarine

Place chicken in baking dish. Place 1 slice cheese on top of each breast. Mix together soup and wine; pour over chicken. Sprinkle herbed dressing on top of chicken. Dribble melted margarine on top of dressing. Bake at 350 degrees for one hour.

Serves 6

VEAL PARMIGIANA

4 tenderized veal cutlets
2 tablespoons salad oil
1 6-ounce can tomato paste
1 tablespoon sugar
1 tablespoon sweet basil
4 whole black peppercorns
1 egg, beaten
1/4 teaspoon pepper
3 tablespoons grated Parmesan cheese
4 tablespoons salad oil
4 slices mozzarella cheese
1 green onion, chopped
1 8-ounce can tomato sauce
1 tablespoon oregano
1 tablespoon garlic salt
1 1/2 cups boiling water
1/2 teaspoon salt
1/2 cup fine bread crumbs

Heat salad oil. Add and cook the green onion. Add tomato paste and sauce and cook 5 minutes, stirring constantly. Add sugar, oregano, basil, garlic salt, peppercorns, and water and simmer 30 minutes. (This much can be done the day before serving and kept in the refrigerator.) Dip veal in egg, salt, bread crumbs, and cheese. Brown well and place in a single layer in pan and pour sauce over meat. Bake covered at 350 degrees for 1 hour. Top with mozzarella cheese and bake 10 more minutes.

Serves 4

COFFEE FLAVORED POT ROAST

1 package instant meat marinade
2/3 cup cold coffee
1 medium garlic clove, minced or pressed
1/4 teaspoon sweet basil
3 to 4 pounds beef pot roast (any favorite cut)
1 10 1/2-ounce can condensed cream of mushroom soup
1 large onion, sliced

Pour contents of instant meat marinade package into Dutch oven with tight-fitting lid. Add coffee and blend thoroughly. Blend in garlic and basil. Place meat in marinade. Pierce all surfaces of meat deeply and thoroughly with fork. Marinate 15 minutes, turning several times. Add soup and onion; blend with marinade. Cook over low heat, turning meat once. When liquid begins to bubble, reduce heat. Cover tightly; simmer until tender, approximately 2 to 2 1/2 hours. Remove from gravy to hot platter. Thicken gravy if desired. Slice meat; serve gravy separately.

Serves 6

Vegetables

CELERY ALMANDINE

1/3 cup sliced almonds	1 teaspoon Accent
2 tablespoons butter	1/2 teaspoon sugar
4 cups diagonally sliced celery	1/8 teaspoon garlic powder
1 chicken bouillon cube, crumbled	1/8 teaspoon ground ginger

Saute almonds in butter; add remaining ingredients. Stir until mixed; cover and cook 10 minutes until celery is tender and crisp.

Serves 4 to 6

YELLOW SQUASH

3 pounds sliced yellow squash	1/4 can water
1 medium sliced onion	1 can mushroom soup
1 can drained water chestnuts	salt to taste
1 can mushrooms	pepper to taste
1/2 cup Pepperidge Farm seasoned dressing crumbs	1/2 cup sliced almonds

Parboil squash until tender. Mix squash, onions, water chestnuts, mushrooms, and dressing with mushroom soup that has been diluted with 1/4 can water, seasoning mixture with salt and pepper to taste. Bake at 325 degrees for 20 minutes. Sprinkle sliced almonds on top of squash. Continue to bake for 10 minutes.

Serves 6 to 8

BAKED ACORN SQUASH

3 medium acorn squash
salt to taste
2 tablespoons butter or margarine
1 8 1/4-ounce can crushed pineapple, drained

1 1/4 cups peeled, chopped cooking apple
2 tablespoons brown sugar
1 tablespoon butter or margarine

Cut squash in half; remove seeds. Place cut side down in a shallow baking dish. Add 1/2" boiling water. Bake at 350 degrees for 40 minutes. Turn cut side up, and sprinkle with salt; set aside. Melt 1 tablespoon butter; add pineapple, apple, and sugar, mixing well. Spoon mixture into squash shells. Dot each shell with 1/2 teaspoon butter. Return to oven; bake 30 minutes. *Serves 6*

GREEN CHILI SOUFFLE

1 10-ounce package Fritos
1 can cream of chicken soup
1/2 can green chili peppers, chopped

1 small onion, finely chopped
3/4 can evaporated milk
1 small box Velveeta cheese

Put Fritos in bottom of 8" square baking dish. Mix soup, chili peppers, onion, and evaporated milk together and pour over Fritos. Cover with Velveeta cheese that has been broken into small pieces. Bake 30 to 45 minutes in a 350-degree oven. Ingredients will be soupy when hot, so let cool slightly before serving. *Serves 4*

GREEN CHILI HOMINY

2 cans white hominy
1 4-ounce can green chilies, chopped
1 can cream of mushroom soup, undiluted

1 cup grated cheddar cheese
1/2 teaspoon garlic salt

Mix ingredients. Place in buttered 1 quart casserole. Bake at 350 degrees for 45 minutes. *Serves 4*

SPINACH SOUFFLE BAKED IN SQUASH

4 medium acorn squash
2 tablespoons butter, melted
1 teaspoon ground nutmeg

2 12-ounce packages frozen spinach souffle, thawed

Cut squash in half crosswise. Discard seeds and strings; brush cut surfaces with butter. Arrange cut-side down in large shallow baking dish; add hot water just to cover bottom of pan. Bake at 375 degrees for 20 minutes. Turn squash cut side up; mound spinach souffle in cavities; sprinkle with nutmeg. Bake 40 minutes longer until squash is tender and souffle is set and golden brown, adding more water to pan if necessary.

Serves 8

BLACK-EYED PEA STEW

1 pound (2 cups) dry black-eyed peas
6 cups water
1 6-ounce can tomato paste
1/4 cup red wine vinegar
1 medium onion, chopped
2 cloves garlic, minced or pressed
1 bell pepper, seeded and chopped

2 carrots, scraped and chopped
2 large tomatoes, chopped
1 teaspoon oregano, crushed
3/4 teaspoon salt
1/2 teaspoon sugar
1/4 teaspoon freshly ground black pepper
1/4 teaspoon crushed red pepper

Combine all ingredients and bring to boil. Reduce heat and simmer, covered, for 1 1/2 to 2 hours, or until peas are tender.

Serves 8

Breads

90-MINUTE PECAN CORNBREAD

4 cups all-purpose flour
1 cup yellow cornmeal
1/3 cup sugar
1 1/2 teaspoons salt
1 package active dry yeast
1 cup milk
1/2 cup water
1/2 cup butter or margarine
2 eggs at room temperature
3/4 cup pecan pieces

Combine flour and cornmeal. In large bowl thoroughly mix 2 cups flour mixture, sugar, salt, and undissolved yeast. In saucepan, combine milk, water, and butter. Heat over low heat until liquids are very warm (120 to 130 degrees). Gradually add to dry ingredients and beat 2 minutes at medium speed of electric mixer, scraping bowl occasionally. Add eggs and 1/2 cup water mixture until well blended. Beat at high speed 2 minutes, scraping bowl occasionally. Stir in pecan pieces and remaining flour mixture until well blended. Batter will be stiff. Divide batter between 2 greased 8" round pans. Cover; let rise in warm place, free from drafts, until doubled in bulk—about 45 minutes. Bake at 375 degrees for 30 minutes or until done. Remove from pans and cool on wire racks. Serve warm or cold.

Makes two 8" round loaves

APRICOT NUT BREAD

2 cups pancake mix
1/2 cup firmly packed brown sugar
1/2 cup chopped dried apricots
1/2 cup chopped pecans
2 teaspoons grated orange peel
1 teaspoon cinnamon
1 1/4 cups milk
3 eggs, beaten
3 tablespoons butter or margarine, melted
1 teaspoon vanilla

Heat oven to 350 degrees. Grease a loaf pan; line bottom with wax paper; grease wax paper. Combine pancake mix, brown sugar, apricots, pecans, orange peel and cinnamon in large bowl. Add milk, eggs, butter, and vanilla; stir lightly until moistened. Pour into prepared pan. Bake 55 to 60 minutes. Cool about 10 minutes. Remove from pan onto wire rack. Cool thoroughly before wrapping. NOTE: Bread slices better if made the day before slicing.

Serves 6 to 8

MELT-IN-YOUR-MOUTH BISCUITS

1 cup whole wheat flour
1/4 teaspoon salt
2 teaspoons baking powder

2/3 cup light cream
2 1/2 teaspoons sour cream

Sift together flour, salt, and baking powder. Gradually stir in cream with a fork. Then add sour cream. Drop 6 portions 3" apart on ungreased cookie sheet. Bake at 450 degrees for 12 to 15 minutes.

Serves 3

PERFECT POPOVERS

1 1/4 cups flour
1 1/4 cups milk
3 eggs

pinch salt
olive oil
popover pan

Preheat oven to 450 degrees. Beat eggs with whip or hand mixer until foamy and lemon colored. Add milk (at room temperature) and stir until just blended. Add flour all at once. Hand beat until foamy and smooth. Grease popover pan lightly. Pour batter into a pitcher and fill pan. If using traditional muffin pan, fill every other hole. Bake at 450 degrees for 15 minutes. Reduce heat to 350 degrees and bake for 30 minutes. Remove popovers with a sharp knife and serve hot. CAUTION: Do not open oven door to check popovers or they will fall.

Serves 6

MINI-MORSEL MUFFINS

2 cups white flour
1/2 of 12-ounce package semi-sweet mini-chocolate chips
1/2 cup chopped nuts
1 tablespoon baking powder
1/2 teaspoon salt

3/4 cup milk
6 tablespoons butter, melted
1/4 cup firmly packed brown sugar
2 eggs
1 teaspoon vanilla extract

Preheat oven to 400 degrees. In a large bowl, combine flour, chocolate chips, nuts, baking powder, and salt. In a small bowl, blend milk, melted butter, brown sugar, eggs, and vanilla. Add to flour mixture. Stir just until dry ingredients are moistened—batter may be lumpy. Spoon into greased or paper lined 2 1/2" muffin pans. Bake for 20 minutes. Cool in pans 5 minutes; remove from pans. Serve warm or cool completely.

Makes 12 muffins

SOUR CREAM PANCAKES

2 1/2 cups flour
1 tablespoon baking powder
1 teaspoon salt
1 tablespoon sugar
3 eggs

2 teaspoons baking soda
2 cups buttermilk
2 tablespoons butter or margarine, melted
1 cup sour cream

Dissolve baking soda in buttermilk and let stand until needed. Sift together dry ingredients. Beat eggs. Add flour mixture and buttermilk mixture and sour cream to eggs alternately, beating gently until smooth. Last, fold in melted butter. Cook on hot, lightly greased grill. Serve with melted butter and maple syrup. NOTE: Recipe can be halved, using 2 eggs.

Makes 18 large pancakes

SWEDISH PANCAKES

3 eggs
2 cups milk
1 cup flour

1 tablespoon sugar
1 teaspoon salt

Combine all ingredients and beat with rotary beater until smooth. Batter will be very thin. Heat pancake griddle. Melt enough butter to cover griddle. Then pour about 1/3 cup batter onto griddle, tilting griddle until it is coated. Brown cakes on both sides—edges should be lacy. Roll up cakes immediately. They may be unrolled when spread with butter and syrups and then re-rolled.

Serves 4

EBELSKIEVERS

1 1/3 cups milk
1 1/3 cups flour
3 eggs, separated
2 teaspoons baking powder

1/2 teaspoon salt
1 teaspoon sugar
1/4 cup melted margarine

Sift dry ingredients together. Mix together milk, margarine, and beaten egg yolks; add to dry ingredients, stirring until blended. Beat egg whites until stiff. Fold egg whites into mixture, stirring sparingly. Put heaping tablespoon mixture in hot greased Ebelskiever tins or cook on greased pancake griddle.

Serves 4

Desserts

PEANUT BUTTER BALLS

4 sticks butter	1 cup ground pecans
2 boxes powdered sugar	2 1/2 6-ounce packages semi-sweet chocolate chips
1 quart extra crunchy peanut butter	1 block paraffin

Mix first four ingredients and roll into balls 1" in diameter. Chill until firm. Melt chocolate chips and paraffin in double boiler. Leave over hot water while dipping balls. Insert a toothpick into a ball and dip into chocolate. Drain on wax paper.

Makes 150 balls

TOLL HOUSE COOKIE BRITTLE

1 cup margarine	1 6-ounce package semi-sweet chocolate chips
1 1/2 teaspoons vanilla	
1 teaspoon salt	1 cup sugar
2 cups sifted flour	1/2 cup finely chopped nuts

Blend margarine, vanilla, and salt. Gradually beat in sugar. Add flour and chocolate chips. Press evenly into ungreased 15x10" pan. Sprinkle nuts over top. Bake in 375 degree oven for 25 minutes. Cool. Then break into pieces and drain on paper towels.

Makes 2 dozen

RANGER COOKIES

1 cup margarine
1 cup sugar
1 cup brown sugar
1 teaspoon vanilla
2 eggs

2 cups flour
1/2 teaspoon baking powder
1 teaspoon soda
2 cups Rice Krispies
2 cups quick oatmeal

Cream margarine and sugar together. Add brown sugar, vanilla, and eggs. Then add flour, baking powder, and soda. Stir in Rice Krispies and oatmeal. Drop by spoonfuls onto ungreased baking sheet; bake at 350 degrees for 12 to 15 minutes. NOTE: You may also add 1 cup coconut, 1 cup nuts, and/or 1 cup chocolate chips.

Makes 6 dozen

WINTER FRUIT SPLENDOR

1 3-ounce package jello lemon *or* lime flavor gelatin *or* sugar-free jello
1/2 cup white grape juice *or* pineapple juice

1 1/2 cups fruit (banana slices, orange sections, seedless grapes, diced apple, pears, or any combination)
3/4 cup boiling water

Dissolve jello in boiling water. Combine fruit juice to make 1 1/4 cups. Add to gelatin, stirring until slightly thickened. Let stand or chill until thickened, about 10 minutes. Add fruit and spoon into dessert glasses. Chill about 1 hour. Garnish as desired. Makes about 3 cups.

Serves 6

APPLE CRISP

4 cups sliced, pared baking apples
1 cup packed brown sugar
1/2 cup flour
1/2 cup dry, uncooked oatmeal
1 teaspoon cinnamon
1 teaspoon nutmeg
6 tablespoons soft butter

Heat oven to 375 degrees. Place apples in greased 8x12" baking pan. Blend sugar, flour, oats, spices, and butter; crumble over apples. Bake 35 minutes—top should be brown. Serve warm with cream or ice cream.
Serves 4

BANANAS BARRON

2 bananas
2 tablespoons butter
2 tablespoons brown sugar
3 tablespoons quality brandy
vanilla ice cream

Melt butter in saucepan; add bananas. Sprinkle brown sugar over bananas. Turn bananas and ladle melting sugar over them. When bananas begin to turn golden, add brandy—do not flame. Serve over ice cream, spoon sugar liquor mixture over ice cream.
Serves 2 to 4

PEACHES OR PEARS CARDINALE

4 ripe peaches *or* 4 ripe pears
1 lemon
2 cups water
2 1/4 cups white sugar
1 teaspoon vanilla extract
1 pint fresh raspberries

Kirsch
1 teaspoon arrowroot flour *or* cornstarch
1/4 pound blanched, slivered almonds

If using pears, peel them carefully, putting them in cold water with a little lemon juice added as you peel them. This keeps them from turning brown. Make a syrup by boiling together 2 cups water and 2 cups sugar for 5 minutes. Add 1 teaspoon vanilla and the peeled pears or unpeeled peaches. Let the fruit simmer for a minute or two. If using peaches, remove them, slip off skins, and return to syrup. Poach until the fruit is tender, but not too soft. Drain and chill fruit.

Mash 1 pint fresh raspberries with 1/4 cup sugar. Add 1 teaspoon arrowroot flour or cornstarch mixed with 2 tablespoons cold water. Simmer and stir for a minute or two until mixture is thick and clear. Rub the puree through a sieve. Add Kirsch to taste. Place the whole peaches or pears upright in crystal bowls; cut a thin slice off the bottom so they will stand. Pour the puree over them and sprinkle with blanched, slivered almonds.

Serves 4

HOLIDAY CRANBERRY CAKE

Topping:
1/2 cup sugar
1/4 cup margarine or butter
1 10-ounce jar (1 cup) red currant jelly
1 cup fresh whole cranberries
1/2 cup chopped nuts

Cake:
1 package spice cake mix
2/3 cup sour cream
1/3 cup oil
1/2 teaspoon cinnamon
1/2 teaspoon nutmeg
3 eggs

Heat oven to 350 degrees. Generously grease two 8" or 9" round cake pans. In small saucepan, combine sugar, margarine, and jelly. Heat until jelly is melted and mixture comes to a boil, stirring constantly. Pour into prepared pans; sprinkle cranberries and nuts over jelly mixture. In large bowl, combine all cake ingredients at low speed until moistened; beat 2 minutes at highest speed. Carefully spoon batter evenly onto top of jelly mixture. Bake at 350 degrees for 30 to 40 minutes or until toothpick inserted in center comes out clean. Remove from pans immediately onto cooling racks; cool 15 minutes before putting layers together with topping sides up. Cool completely. NOTE: Cake may be baked in a 13x9" pan. Bake for 60 to 65 minutes. For a more festive cake, frost sides of cooled cake with sweetened whipped cream. Refrigerate until served.
Serves 12

PEACHES AND CREAM CAKE

1 package white cake mix
1 16-ounce can sliced peaches
1/4 cup peach brandy or brandy
1/4 cup peach preserves
1 4-ounce container frozen prepared whipped topping, thawed

Prepare cake mix according to package directions. Turn into a greased and floured 13x9x2" baking pan. Bake according to package directions. Drain peaches, reserving liquid. Add brandy to liquid. While cake is still warm, prick top of cake with a long-tined fork at 1/2" intervals. Slowly spoon brandy mixture over cake allowing all of the liquid to be absorbed. Carefully spread preserves over top of cake. Halve any large peach slices. Arrange peaches on top of cake. Cool cake. To serve, place dollop of whipped topping on each serving. Store in refrigerator.
Serves 12 to 15

FRESH APPLE CAKE

4 cups apples, chopped coarsely
2 cups sugar
2 eggs
1 cup vegetable oil
2 1/2 cups flour
2 teaspoons soda

1 teaspoon salt
1 teaspoon cinnamon
1 cup pecans, chopped
1 cup powdered sugar
2 tablespoons lemon juice

Preheat oven to 350 degrees. Mix together apples and sugar and let stand in mixing bowl until juicy. Separate eggs. Beat egg whites until stiff. Add egg yolks to apples and sugar and beat. Add vegetable oil and mix. Sift flour, soda, salt, and cinnamon together. Add flour mixture to oil and egg mixture. Mix well. Fold in pecans. Bake in 10" greased and floured bundt pan. Bake cake for 1 1/4 hours. Turn out cake while warm and ice with powdered sugar dissolved in lemon juice.

Serves 10 to 12

CHEESE CAKE

3 8-ounce packages cream cheese
4 eggs
1 teaspoon vanilla
1 3/4 cups sugar

2 cups graham cracker crumbs
3/4 stick margarine
1 pint sour cream
1 teaspoon vanilla

Using an electric mixer, combine the cream cheese, eggs, 1 1/2 cups sugar, and vanilla. Beat for 20 minutes at medium speed. Crush graham crackers and mix with 3/4 stick margarine. Press graham cracker mixture on bottom and sides of springform pan. Carefully pour cream cheese mixture on top of graham crackers, and bake 35 to 40 minutes at 350 degrees. Remove from oven and pour sour cream topping on top and bake for 10 minutes. Prepare sour cream topping by mixing well 1 pint sour cream, 1/4 cup sugar, and 1 teaspoon vanilla. When through baking, open oven door, leaving cake in oven until cool. Refrigerate overnight.

Serves 10

ORANGE PECAN PIE

2 oranges pureed *or* 1/4 cup frozen orange juice concentrate
3 eggs
3/4 cup dark corn syrup
2 tablespoons butter or margarine, melted
1 teaspoon vanilla
1/2 cup sugar (1 cup if using orange juice)
1/8 teaspoon salt
1/2 teaspoon grated orange rind
1 cup pecan halves
1 unbaked 9" pastry shell

To puree oranges, peel, seed and cut oranges into eighths. Then process at medium speed in electric blender to produce 2/3 cup puree. To make pie filling, beat eggs in large bowl; add puree or orange juice; stir in remaining ingredients except pastry shell; blend well. Pour pie mixture into pastry shell. Bake at 400 degrees for 15 minutes. Reduce heat to 350 degrees and bake another 35 to 40 minutes. Filling will be moist in center. Cool.

Serves 6 to 8

FRENCH STRAWBERRY PIE

1 9" baked pie shell
1 3-ounce package cream cheese
3 tablespoons cream
1 quart strawberries
1 cup sugar
1 cup whipping cream
2 tablespoons cornstarch
few drops lemon juice

Blend the cream cheese and cream until soft and smooth. Spread over the cooled pie shell. Wash and hull the berries; select one half of the best ones. If they are large, slice in half. Add the sugar to the rest of berries and let stand until juicy. Mash and run through a sieve. Mix this puree with the cornstarch; add a few drops of lemon juice. Cook this mixture until thick and transparent, stirring constantly. Cool and put half the pureed mixture over the cream cheese. Put the halved berries in the remaining sauce and pour over the berries in the pie shell. Chill. Serve with sweetened whipped cream.

Serves 6 to 8

STRAWBERRY PIE

1 9" baked pie shell
3/4 cup sugar
4 tablespoons cornstarch
4 tablespoons strawberry jello

3 tablespoons white Karo syrup
1 cup water
1 1/2 pints sliced strawberries
1/2 cup chopped pecans

Cook sugar, cornstarch, jello, syrup, and water until thick. When cool, add strawberries and chopped pecans. Pour into baked pie crust.

Serves 6 to 8

KEY LIME MACADAMIA DREAM PIE

1 cup shortbread cookie crumbs
1/2 cup finely chopped macadamia nuts plus 1/2 cup coarsely chopped macadamia nuts
1/4 cup sugar
5 tablespoons butter, melted
4 egg yolks

1 14-ounce can sweetened condensed milk
1 3-ounce package cream cheese, softened
1/2 cup freshly squeezed key lime juice (may substitute Persian limes)
1 cup whipping cream

To make crust, combine cookie crumbs, finely chopped nuts, sugar, and melted butter. Press into a lightly greased 9" pie plate using the back of a spoon. Chill. Using a whisk or electric mixer, combine egg yolks with condensed milk. Add cream cheese and beat until thoroughly combined. Add lime juice gradually to incorporate. Pour mixture into chilled crust and refrigerate overnight. Just before serving, whip cream until stiff. With a pastry bag, pipe large swirls of whipped cream around the edge of the pie. Sprinkle with macadamia nuts and serve.

Serves 8

FRENCH SILK PIE

2 squares unsweetened chocolate
3/4 cup butter
1 cup plus 1 tablespoon sugar
1 teaspoon vanilla
3 eggs
1 9" baked pie shell
1/2 pint whipping cream
chocolate shavings

Melt and cool chocolate; cream butter and sugar. Add chocolate and vanilla and mix thoroughly. Add one egg at a time, beating 4 minutes per egg on medium speed. Pour mixture into cooled pie shell. Top pie with whipped cream and shave chocolate over top. Refrigerate several hours.

Serves 6 to 8

MISCELLANEOUS RECIPES

Peach and Raspberry Jam

Praline Sauce

Toffee-Fudge Sauce

Caramel Pecan Sauce

Steak Marinade

Smooth-n-Easy Gravy

Salsa Pronto

Homemade Chicken Broth

Orange Dressing for Fruits

Whipped Cream Waldorf Salad Dressing

Sunflower Salad Dressing

Winter Cocoa Mix

Russian Tea Mix

Ritz Bits Treats

PEACH AND RASPBERRY JAM

1 box red raspberries, crushed
1 1/2 pounds *or* 2 cups peaches, ground
4 3/4 cups sugar
3/4 cup water
1 box pectin jell (pen or sure-jell)

Mix crushed raspberries, peaches, and sugar in a large bowl. Mix water and pectin in saucepan and bring to a boil; boil one minute. Stir into first mixture and mix for 3 minutes. Fill jars and set for 24 hours. Then freeze. NOTE: This jam is delicious on vanilla ice cream.

PRALINE SAUCE

1 cup water
2/3 cup chopped pecans
1/2 cup dark corn syrup
1/2 cup firmly packed brown sugar
1 tablespoon butter or margarine

Bring water to a boil in a small saucepan; add chopped pecans, reduce heat, and cook mixture about 5 minutes. Drain and set aside. Combine brown sugar, syrup, and butter in a heavy saucepan. Bring mixture to a boil; reduce heat, and simmer 5 minutes, stirring constantly. Stir in pecans. Serve warm over ice cream.

Makes 1 cup

TOFFEE FUDGE SAUCE

1 14-ounce bag caramels
1/2 cup milk chocolate chips
1/4 cup strong coffee
1/4 cup milk

Combine all ingredients in a saucepan; cook over medium heat, stirring occasionally, until chocolate chips and caramels melt. Serve warm over pound cake or ice cream. NOTE: One 12 1/4-ounce jar caramel sauce may be substituted for bag of caramels.

Makes 2 cups

CARAMEL PECAN SAUCE

2/3 cup sugar
1/4 cup corn syrup
1 cup water
1 cup heavy cream
1 cup toasted pecans

Bring sugar, corn syrup, and water to boil in small saucepan. Continue cooking until dark golden color, 15 to 20 minutes. Remove from heat. Slowly whisk in cream. Mixture will thicken and lump up. Return to heat, stirring constantly, and continue cooking until smooth. Remove from heat and stir in pecans. Allow to cool and thicken before serving. This sauce may be reheated by putting in bowl over pan of boiling water or by setting sauce in bowl inside pan of warm, not boiling, water and stirring. Sauce should not be reheated to very high temperature—it should just be slightly warm. Serve over ice cream.

Makes 2 1/2 cups

STEAK MARINADE

1/2 cup pineapple juice
1/2 cup soy sauce
1/2 cup sherry

Mix ingredients and pour over steak of your choice. Marinate steak for 24 hours. Broil or grill steak to required doneness.

Makes 1 1/2 cups

SMOOTH 'N EASY GRAVY

2 tablespoons fat (meat drippings)
2 tablespoons flour
1 cup cold water, milk or broth
salt to taste
pepper to taste

Measure meat drippings into pan. Sprinkle flour evenly over drippings and pour cold liquid over it. Stir to blend thoroughly; return to heat and bring to a boil, stirring constantly. Boil 1 minute. Add seasonings to taste.

Makes 1 cup medium pan gravy

SALSA PRONTO

1 14 1/2-ounce can Del Monte mexican style stewed tomatoes
1/2 cup finely chopped onion
2 tablespoons finely chopped cilantro
2 teaspoons lemon juice
1 small clove garlic, minced
1/8 teaspoon hot pepper sauce

Place tomatoes in blender container. Cover and run on lowest speed 2 seconds to chop tomatoes. Combine with onion, cilantro, lemon juice, garlic, and pepper sauce. Add additional pepper sauce, if desired. Serve with tortilla chips.

Makes 2 cups

HOMEMADE CHICKEN BROTH

2 pounds chicken bones
3 quarts water
1 cup sliced onions
3/4 cup *each* sliced carrots and celery
10 peppercorns
5 parsley stems
1 bay leaf
4 whole cloves
1/8 teaspoon thyme leaves

Combine all ingredients. Bring to a boil; reduce heat. Simmer 2 1/2 hours. Strain to remove solids. Refrigerate until fat hardens on top. Discard fat. Serve with saltines or oyster crackers for a terrific snack.

Makes 10 cups

ORANGE DRESSING FOR FRUITS

1 6-ounce can frozen concentrated orange juice undiluted
3/4 cup salad oil
1/4 cup cider vinegar
3 tablespoons sugar
1/2 teaspoon dry mustard
1/4 teaspoon salt
1/8 teaspoon liquid red pepper sauce

Shake or beat together all ingredients, or mix in electric blender. Cover and store in refrigerator. Shake well before using.

Makes 1 3/4 cups

WHIPPED CREAM WALDORF SALAD DRESSING

1/4 cup mayonnaise
1 tablespoon sugar
1/2 teaspoon lemon juice
dash salt
1/2 cup whipping cream *or* 1 cup prepared whipped topping

Whip whipping cream. Combine mayonnaise, sugar, lemon juice, and salt. Fold whipping cream or prepared whipped topping into mayonnaise mixture.

Makes 1 1/2 cups

SUNFLOWER SALAD DRESSING

5 cups oil
2 cups vinegar
1 pound honey
1 1/2 ounces salt
3/4 ounce ground white pepper
1/4 ounce chopped freeze-dried chives
1 pound sugar
2 1/2 ounces granulated garlic
4 ounces roasted sunflower seeds

Add ingredients to mixer in order given. Mix at medium speed. Stir in sunflower seeds.

Makes 10 cups

WINTER COCOA MIX

1 16-ounce package instant chocolate flavored mix
1 6-ounce jar non-dairy coffee creamer
1 cup sifted powdered sugar
1 25.6-ounce package instant nonfat dry milk powder

Combine all ingredients, stirring well. Store in a covered container. To serve, combine 1/3 cup mix and 1 cup boiling water for each serving; stir well.

Makes 36 servings

RUSSIAN TEA MIX

3 cups sugar
2 cups Tang orange drink
1 cup instant tea
1 teaspoon ground cloves
1 teaspoon cinnamon
1 package Wyler lemonade mix

Mix dry ingredients in blender and store in tightly sealed jar. NOTE: Use 3 teaspoons per tall glass of water.

Makes 6 cups of mix

RITZ BITS TREATS

2 boxes Ritz Bits crackers
2 cups dry roasted peanuts
1/2 cup butter or margarine
1 cup granulated white sugar
1/2 cup white Karo syrup
1 teaspoon vanilla
1 teaspoon baking soda

Combine crackers and peanuts and place on two large, Pam-sprayed roasting pans. Bring to a boil the butter, sugar, and Karo syrup. Let boil 5 minutes. Remove from heat and add vanilla and soda, stirring well. Pour mixture over crackers and peanuts. Bake in a 300 degree oven for one hour, stirring every 15 minutes. When finished baking, pour onto wax paper and let cool. Break mixture apart and store in an airtight container.

Makes 9 cups

POTPOURRI

Helpful Hints

Gift Ideas

Cooking a Turkey

Microwave Shortcuts

Helpful Hints

1. Plan 1/4 to 1/2 pound cheese per person.

2. Serve cheese at room temperature. Take soft cheese out of refrigerator half an hour ahead; hard cheese two to three hours. To prevent cheese from drying out, leave it in its wrapper.

3. Do not put strong cheese next to mild ones.

4. Sprinkle pear, apple wedges and bananas with lemon juice to keep fruit white.

5. To reheat biscuits, put them in a well dampened paper bag. Twist it closed, put in an oven heated to 300 degrees.

6. If you don't have copper cleaner, use toothpaste and damp cloth.

7. Shake raisins and other dried fruits with flour before adding them to dough or puddings so they won't sink to the bottom during baking.

8. Don't wash greens before you refrigerate them unless you are going to use them the same day. They keep better cold when the leaves are dry.

9. If juice from a fruit pie runs over in the oven (not the self-cleaning type), shake a little salt on it which causes the juice to burn to a crisp so it can be removed easily.

10. Keep a pastry brush or toothbrush handy to brush lemon rind, cheese, onion, or whatever out of the grater before washing it. Good for cleaning rotary beaters and chopper blades, too.

11. To keep egg yolks from crumbling when slicing hard cooked eggs, wet the knife before each cut.

12. If cream will not whip, try adding the white of an egg or a little cornstarch or cream of tartar.

13. To keep spaghetti and macaroni from boiling over, add 1 tablespoon cooking oil or margarine to the water.

14. Brown sugar hard as a rock? Soften by placing a slice of bread in the package and closing it tightly. In a couple of hours, the brown sugar will be soft again. If in a hurry, try grating the amount called for with a hand grater.

15. Unmolding gelatin—Rinse mold pan with cold water. Then coat with salad oil or a thin layer of mayonnaise. Mold will drop out easily.

16. To relieve stomach discomfort caused by eating cooked dried beans, prepare beans as follows: Cover beans with water, bring water to a boil, simmer beans for 20 minutes, turn off heat, and let beans soak in hot water overnight. In the morning, pour water off beans, cover with fresh water, and cook.

17. To hasten avocado ripening, immerse avocado in flour.

18. To prepare coconut, carefully pierce eyes of coconut with screw-driver or ice pick; drain liquid. Place coconut in pan. Heat at 350 degrees for 15 to 30 minutes or until cracks appear. Remove from oven; cool. Tap with hammer to open. Pare off dark skin with vegetable peeler.

19. To keep lettuce several weeks, remove core by rapping it on a counter and twisting or cutting it out. Rinse head and drain very well. Wrap tightly and refrigerate.

20. Food you want to freeze should be wrapped in airtight, moisture-proof material to prevent odors from penetrating the freezer and foods. Date frozen food to determine when they should be used. When defrosting frozen foods, allow enough time to do so in the refrigerator. Do not refreeze food after it has thawed. Foods not suitable for freezing include: bananas, cabbage, celery, cucumbers, mayonnaise, onions, pears, processed meats, radishes, salad greens, tomatoes, whites of hard-cooked eggs.

21. Casserole dishes should be slightly undercooked if they are to be frozen. The cooking process will be completed when the dish is reheated. The following tip will keep dishes from being lost in the freezer. Line casserole dish with heavy foil, then pour partially cooked casserole into foil-lined dish. Cool before freezing. After the casserole is frozen solid, remove the dish. Wrap tightly with foil; label and date the contents. Return foil wrapped casserole to the freezer. When you are ready to prepare the casserole, remove the foil and reheat in the original casserole dish.

Gift Ideas

Holiday Packaging Ideas:

Package a loaf of bread for giving by tying a bright bandanna around the loaf.

A loaf of bread is always welcome in a basket with a special napkin and bow.

Bread is also attractive placed on a cutting board and wrapped tightly in cellophane and a bow. For a special friend, a good bread knife might also be attached.

A cake placed on a pretty tray and covered with clear wrap makes a nice gift after the cake is long gone.

Any canister will hold lots of cookies. You might wish to decorate the outside with polka dot ribbon or ball fringe.

Cookies wrapped in clear wrap and placed in a wire colander promise a gift that will be appreciated for years to come.

Place cookies on a new cookie sheet and wrap with clear wrap for giving to one of your favorite cooks.

A large sea shell filled with nuts or mints and covered with clear wrap makes a beautiful gift.

Fill a wooden or bright plastic sugar scoop with nuts or candy and cover with clear wrap. Tie with a huge bright bow.

Use small buckets to put nuts or mints in and place bow on handle.

Use tin buckets and watering cans to make delightful containers for small items such as rum balls.

A couple of egg cups look adorable filled with candy.

A recipe box (lucite would be nice) filled with candy or nuts would be a lovely gift for a friend who loves to cook. You may want to include your recipe.

Parfait glasses make ideal containers for candy, nuts, or sesame sticks.

Crockery bowls or coffee mugs are great containers for spreads, preserves, and jellies. If necessary, simply seal top with paraffin or cover with clear wrap.

Put syrups and other liquids in old fashioned bottles which are the rage at flea markets everywhere or at your favorite container store.

Be creative, almost anything can be made into a lovely and/or useful container for a gift.

Cooking a Turkey

Roasting Whole Turkey

Place whole turkey, breast side up on rack in shallow roasting pan. If bird is not stuffed, do not truss. Brush with butter or margarine, if desired. Basting is not usually necessary but bird may be basted with pan drippings or melted butter or margarine. If meat thermometer is used, insert so tip of thermometer is in center of inside of thigh muscle. Be sure tip does not touch bone. Roast in moderate oven (325 degrees) until done. (See timetable for approximate roasting time and temperature.)

After skin becomes light golden brown, place loose tent of aluminum foil over legs and breast or cover with thin cloth moistened in melted fat. Do not tuck cloth or foil in around turkey. Do not cover pan. If desired, turkey may be covered with cloth or foil before beginning to roast.

When turkey is two-thirds done, cut band of skin or cord at tail to release legs and allow heat to reach heavy meated part of bird. It is best to start roasting turkey 30 to 45 minutes ahead of schedule. This helps avoid delay if turkey should take longer to cook than time estimated according to timetable. Extra time is also needed to allow bird to stand after cooking so it is easier to carve.

Timetable for Roasting Whole Turkey that is completely thawed.
If bird is unstuffed, time will be 1 to 3 minutes less per pound. Cook to an internal Temperature of 180 to 185 degrees.

Ready-to-Cook Weight Pounds	Approximate Total Roasting Time at 325 Degrees
6 to 8	3 to 3 1/2 hours
8 to 12	3 1/2 to 4 1/2 hours
12 to 16	4 1/2 to 5 1/2 hours
16 to 20	5 1/2 to 6 1/2 hours
20 to 24	6 1/2 to 7 hours

Roasted Whole Turkey Doneness Test

The best indication of doneness is when a meat thermometer inserted in the thigh muscle registers 180 to 185 degrees. If the bird is stuffed, the point of the thermometer should be in the center of the stuffing, and the turkey is done when the thermometer registers 165 degrees. Without a meat thermometer, the doneness of the meat may be judged by whether the drumstick can be moved up and down easily and whether the thigh meat or thickest part of the drumstick feels very soft when pressed between protected fingers.

Foil-Wrapped Turkey

Prepare turkey as for open pan roasting, laying wings flat against sides rather than tucking wing tips under back. Use heavy duty foil large enough to cover bird with 3" overlap and allow 3" to 4" turn up at each end. Turkeys up to 15 pounds may be placed lengthwise on single sheet of 18" foil. Join two sheets of 14" or 18" foil for larger birds.

Place prepared turkey on its back in center of foil. Place small folds of foil over ends of legs, wing tips and tail to prevent puncturing outside wrap. Bring long ends of foil up over breast of turkey and overlap 3". Close ends by folding up 3" to 4" so drippings will not run out of package. Wrap loosely and do not seal airtight. Do not use more foil than necessary to cover turkey.

Place wrapped turkey, breast up, in shallow pan. Roast in hot oven (450 degrees) until done. See roasting chart for foil-wrapped turkey and doneness test. Open foil one or two times during roasting to judge progress. When thigh joint and breast meat begin to soften, fold foil back completely to allow turkey to brown. If desired, insert meat thermometer at this time.

Timetable for Roasting Foil-Wrapped Turkey that is completely thawed. Cook to an Internal Temperature of 180 to 185 degrees.

Ready-to-Cook Weight Pounds	Approximate Total Roasting Time at 325 Degrees
7 to 9	2 1/4 to 2 1/2 hours
10 to 13	2 3/4 to 3 hours
14 to 17	3 1/2 to 4 hours
18 to 21	4 1/2 to 5 hours
22 to 24	5 1/2 to 6 hours

Microwave Shortcuts

Micro-Baked Potatoes

Cook at HIGH	1 medium (6 to 7 ounces)	4 to 6 minutes
	2 medium	7 to 8 minutes
	4 medium	12 to 14 minutes

Rinse potatoes; pat dry; prick several times with fork. Arrange potatoes in microwave oven, leaving 1" between each. Microwave at HIGH until done, turning and rearranging potatoes once. Let potatoes stand 5 minutes before serving.

Melting Chocolate Squares

Cook at Medium 50% Power	1 to 2 squares	1 1/2 to 2 minutes
	3 squares	2 minutes
	4 to 5 squares	2 to 2 1/2 minutes
	16 squares	2 1/2 to 3 minutes

Place chocolate squares in a small bowl; microwave at MEDIUM until melted, stirring once.

Cooking Ground Beef

Cook at HIGH	1 1/2 pound	2 to 3 minutes
	2 pounds	4 to 6 minutes
	2 1/2 pounds	6 to 8 minutes
	3 pounds	8 to 10 minutes

Crumble beef into a baking dish. Cover with wax paper, and microwave at HIGH until no longer pink, stirring at 2-minute intervals. Drain well.

Melting Butter

Cook at HIGH	1 to 2 tablespoons	35 to 45 seconds
	3 tablespoons	50 to 55 seconds
	1/4 to 1/2 cup	1 minute
	3/4 cup	1 to 1 1/2 minutes
	1 cup	1 1/2 to 2 minutes

Place butter in a 2-cup glass measure; microwave at HIGH until melted.

Melting Chocolate Chips

Cook at MEDIUM	1/2 to 1 cup	2 to 3 minutes
50% Power	1 1/2 cups	3 to 3 1/2 minutes
	2 cups	3 1/2 to 4 minutes

Place chocolate chips in one-quart mixing bowl; microwave at MEDIUM until melted, stirring once.

Cooking Chicken

Cook at HIGH	1 skinned, boned breast half-5 oz.	3 to 4 minutes
	2 skinned, boned breast halves	4 to 5 minutes
	4 skinned, boned breast halves	8 to 10 minutes
	1 3-pound fryer, cut up, skinned	9 to 10 minutes

Place chicken in a baking dish. Cover and microwave at HIGH until tender and done, giving dish a half-turn and rearranging chicken after half the cooking time.

Toasting Nuts

Cook at HIGH	1/4 cup chopped nuts	3 minutes
	1/2 cup chopped nuts	3 1/2 minutes
	1 cup chopped nuts	4 to 5 minutes

Spread nuts on a pie plate or a glass pizza plate. Microwave at HIGH until toasted; stir at 2-minute intervals.

Cooking Bacon

Cook at HIGH	1 slice	1 to 2 minutes
	2 slices	2 to 3 minutes
	4 slices	3 1/2 to 4 1/2 minutes
	6 slices	5 to 7 minutes

Place bacon on a microwave-safe rack in a 12x8x2" baking dish; cover with paper towels. Microwave at HIGH until bacon is crisp. Drain bacon.

Softening Butter or Margarine

Cook at LOW	1 to 2 tablespoons	15 to 30 seconds
10% Power	3 tablespoons	30 to 45 seconds
	1/4 to 1/2 cup	1 to 1 1/4 minutes
	1 cup	1 1/2 to 1 3/4 minutes

Place butter on a microwave-safe plate; microwave at LOW until soft.

Rising Yeast Dough

Cook at	using 1 to 2 cups flour	1 1/2 minutes
MEDIUM LOW	using 2 to 3 cups flour	2 minutes
30% Power	using 3 or more cups flour	2 1/2 minutes

Place dough in a large, greased microwave-safe bowl, turning to grease all sides. Cover dough loosely with wax paper, and place in oven. Microwave at MEDIUM LOW according to chart; let stand 5 minutes. Repeat microwaving and standing 2 to 4 times until dough has doubled in bulk.

Hard-Cooked Eggs

Cook at **MEDIUM**	1 egg	1 1/4 to 1 1/2 minutes
50% Power	2 eggs	1 3/4 to 2 1/4 minutes
	3 eggs	3 3/4 to 4 1/4 minutes

Break eggs into lightly greased individual custard cups or microwave-safe coffee cups; pierce each yolk with a wooden pick. Cover with heavy-duty plastic wrap, and microwave at MEDIUM to desired degree of doneness, turning cups halfway through cooking time. Let eggs stand, covered, 1 1/2 to 2 1/2 minutes. Use eggs prepared this way in potato salad, egg salad, or other dishes that use cooked eggs. Do not use eggs prepared this way for deviled eggs.

INDEX

A

Almond Cinnamon Cookies, 10
Almond Joy Cake, 68
Almond Tea, 129
Appetizers
  Arkansas Hot Pepper Pecans, 6
  Broiled Grapefruit, 131
  Cheese Straws, 99
  Cheese Strips, 22
  Chex Party Mix, 6
  Ham and Cheese Rolls, 131
  Hot Dogs in Sweet and
    Sour Sauce, 91
  Oriental Hot Munch, 99
  Pecan Cheese Ball, 100
  Ritz Bits Treats, 167
  Salmon Party Roll, 131
  Dips
    Chili Beef Dip, 59
    Fiesta Dip, 59
    Guacamole, 59
    Ham Dip, 5
    Knorrs Spinach Dip, 15
    Lipton California Dip, 5
    Tasty Vegetable Dip, 5
    Tex-Mex Dip, 51
Apple, Apricot, Currant, and
  Pecan Stuffing, 84
Apple Crisp, 155
Apricot Nectar Cake, 42
Apricot Nut Bread, 110, 149
Apricot Pound Cake, 103
Arkansas Hot Pepper Pecans, 6

B

Backyard Coleslaw, 52
Baked Acorn Squash, 147
Baked Beans, 67
Banana Punch, 4
Banana Split Squares, 37
Bananas Barron, 155
Beans
  Baked Beans, 67
  French Bean Casserole, 85
  Green Bean Casserole, 36
  Marinated Beans, 23
  Party Green Beans, 117
Beef
  Beef Stroganoff, 139
  Brisket, 52
  Coffee-Flavored Pot
    Roast, 145
  Easy Day Stew, 136
  Ground Beef Special, 139
  Horseradish Roast, 23
  Lasagna, 141
  Meatloaf Supreme, 140
  Sukiyaki, 142
  Talerine, 46
Beef Stroganoff, 139
Beverage Mixes
  Russian Tea Mix, 167
  Winter Cocoa Mix, 167
Beverages
  Almond Tea, 129
  Banana Punch, 4
  Coffee Ole, 18

Coffee with Cinnamon
  Stick, 107
Collegiate Tea Punch, 45
Eggnog, 107
Fruit Punch, 15
Fruit Slush Punch, 107
Hot Cinnamon Apple
  Punch, 115
Hot Cranberry Punch, 82
Hot Mulled Pineapple, 98
Hot Orange Cider, 72
Hot Punch, 93
Hot Spiced Punch, 4
Jello Punch, 65
Lemonade with Frozen
  Tea Cubes, 130
Mint Julep, 129
Mock Margarita, 58
Open House Punch, 98
Punch with a "Punch", 51
St. Patrick's Punch, 28
Sangria Punch, 58
Smoothie, 40
Spiced Orange Ginger Tea, 91
Strawberry Crush, 129
White Grape Juice Spritzer, 72
Bing Cherry Salad, 134
Black Bean Soup, 136
Blackeyed Peas
  Blackeyed Pea Stew, 148
  Good Luck Blackeyed Peas, 17
Blackeyed Pea Stew, 148
Brandy Cream Pie, 75
Breads
  Apricot Nut Bread, 110, 149
  Brunch Bread, 42
  Cornbread Carrot Biscuits, 93
  Dilly Cheese Bread, 124
  Dinner Rolls, 119

Double Quick Dinner Rolls, 86
Honey Cornmeal Biscuits, 36
Melt-in-Your-Mouth
  Biscuits, 150
Mini-Morsel Muffins, 151
Monkey Bread II, 54
90-Minute Pecan
  Cornbread, 149
Onion-Cheese French
  Bread, 46
Perfect Popovers, 150
Strawberry Bread, 41
Sweet Roll Biscuits, 8
Tupperware Bread, 68
Breakfast and Brunch
  Apricot Nut Bread, 110, 149
  Brunch Bread, 42
  Brunch Egg Casserole, 7
  Coffee with Cinnamon
    Stick, 107
  Do-Ahead Breakfast
    Casserole, 109
  Do-Ahead Sausage Souffle, 40
  Eggnog, 107
  Fruit Slush Punch, 107
  Grit Casserole, 109
  Jalapeno Grits Casserole, 41
  Pineapple Casserole, 40
  Sausage Pinwheels, 109
  Scrumptious Jam Cake
    and Filling, 110
  Sweet Roll Biscuits, 8
  Tangerine Garden Salad, 108
  Winter Spiced Pears and
    Apples, 108
Brisket, 52
Broccoli
  Broccoli Balls, 101
  Broccoli Carrot Casserole, 117

Layered Broccoli Salad, 65
Rice and Broccoli
    Casserole, 53
Broccoli Balls, 101
Broccoli Carrot Casserole, 117
Broiled Grapefruit, 131
Brunch Bread, 42
Brunch Egg Casserole, 7
Buttered Carrots and Celery, 24

C

Cakes
  Almond Joy Cake, 68
  Apricot Nectar Cake, 42
  Apricot Pound Cake, 103
  Cheese Cake, 158
  Chocolate Sheet Cake, 11
  Fresh Apple Cake, 158
  Gingerbread, 74
  Holiday Cranberry Cake, 157
  Milky Way Cake, 73
  Peaches and Cream Cake, 157
  Perfect Chocolate Cake, 17
  Pina Colada Cake, 10
  Pineapple Upside Down
    Cake, 73
  Poppy Seed Cake with Cream
    Filling, 111
  Prune Cake, 102
  Pumpkin Cake, 72
  Scrumptious Jam Cake and
    Filling, 110
  Snowman Cake, 120
  Strawberry Cake, 25
Candied Ham Loaf, 66
Candy
  Crunch Candy, 8
  Peanut Brittle, 9

Peanut Butter Balls, 153
Pound Candy, 9
Strawberry Candy, 25
Whipped Cream Pralines, 62
Caramel Pecan Sauce, 164
Carrots
  Buttered Carrots and
    Celery, 24
  Carrot Slaw, 100
  Snappy Carrots, 53
Carrot Slaw, 100
Casseroles
  Brunch Egg Casserole, 7
  Chicken and Dressing
    Casserole, 143
  Chicken Tetrazzini, 101
  Do-Ahead Breakfast
    Casserole, 109
  Goodbye Turkey
    Casserole, 123
  Jalapeno Grits Casserole, 41
  Lasagna, 141
  Nutty-Baked Chicken, 143
  Pineapple Casserole, 40
  Talerine, 46
  Texas Casserole, 61
  Yummy Baked Chicken with
    Rice, 16
Cauliflower Salad, 34
Celery
  Buttered Carrots and
    Celery, 24
  Celery Amandine, 146
Celery Amandine, 146
Cheese Cake, 158
Cheese Straws, 99
Cheese Strips, 22
Cherry Cream Cheese Pie, 86
Cherry Jello Waldorf Salad, 28
Cherry Salad, 78

Chex Party Mix, 6
Chicken
  Chicken and Dressing
    Casserole, 143
  Chicken Fruit Salad, 133
  Chicken-in-a-Sack, 83
  Chicken Tetrazzini, 101
  Herbed Chicken, 144
  Nutty Baked Chicken, 143
  Southern Shrimp and
    Chicken, 138
  Spicy Chicken with
    Peanuts, 144
  Texas Casserole, 61
  Yummy Baked Chicken with
    Rice, 15
Chicken and Dressing
  Casserole, 143
Chicken Fruit Salad, 133
Chicken-in-a-Sack, 83
Chicken Tetrazzini, 101
Chili Beef Dip, 59
Chocolate
  Almond Joy Cake, 68
  Chocolate Butter Creme
    Frosting, 18
  Chocolate Cream Filling, 18
  Chocolate Fudge Frosting, 111
  Chocolate Layer Squares, 77
  Chocolate Sheet Cake, 11
  Oatmeal Chocolate Chip
    Cookies, 94
  Perfect Chocolate Cake, 17
Chocolate Cream Filling, 18
Chocolate Fudge Frosting, 111
Chocolate Layer Squares, 77
Chocolate Sheet Cake, 11
Classic Waldorf Salad, 132
Clear Tomato Soup, 22
Coffee-Flavored Pot Roast, 145

Coffee Ole, 18
Coffee with Cinnamon Stick, 107
Collegiate Tea Punch, 45
Cookies
  Almond Cinnamon
    Cookies, 10
  Cranberry Cookies, 102
  Oatmeal Chocolate Chip
    Cookies, 94
  Ranger Cookies, 154
  Toll House Cookie Brittle, 153
Company Potatoes, 24
Cooking a Turkey, 173-174
Corn Marinate, 61
Cornbread Carrot Biscuits, 93
Cranberry-Burgundy Glazed
  Ham, 35
Cranberry Cookies, 102
Cranberry Grape Salad, 100
Cranberry Relish Oldtime, 115
Crunch Candy, 8
Crunchy Salad, 115

D

Date Nut Pie, 76
Desserts
  Apple Crisp, 155
  Banana Split Squares, 37
  Bananas Barron, 155
  Chocolate Layer Squares, 77
  Eloquent Dessert of
    Blueberries, 124
  Gingerbread, 74
  Hello Dollies, 77
  Ice Cream Sundae Dessert, 47
  Peaches or Pears
    Cardinale, 156
  PTA Dessert, 54

Whipped Cream Pralines, 62
Winter Fruit Splendor, 154
Winter Spiced Pears and
  Applies, 109
Dijon Potato Salad, 132
Dilly Cheese Bread, 124
Dinner Rolls, 119
Do-Ahead Breakfast
  Casserole, 109
Do-Ahead Sausage Souffle, 40
Double Quick Dinner Rolls, 86
Dressing
  Apple, Apricot, Currant,
    and Pecan Stuffing, 84
  Dressing, 116

E

Easy Day Stew, 136
Easy Millionaire Pie, 75
Ebelskievers, 152
Eggnog, 107
Eloquent Dessert of Blue-
  berries, 124
English Pea Salad, 91

F

Fiesta Dip, 59
Fillings
  Chocolate Cream Filling, 18
  Jam Filling, 110
  Poppy Seed Cream Filling, 111
Fish
  Salmon Loaf, 138
  Southern Shrimp and
    Chicken, 138
Fluffy Mustard Sauce, 66

French Bean Casserole, 85
French Silk Pie, 161
French Strawberry Pie, 159
Fresh Apple Cake, 158
Fresh Fruit Shell Salad, 132
Frostings
  Chocolate Butter Creme
    Frosting, 18
  Chocolate Fudge Frosting, 111
Fruit with Poppy Seed
  Dressing, 7
Fruit Punch, 15
Fruit Slush Punch, 107

G

Garden Salad with Almonds and
  Oranges, 16
Gift Ideas, 171-172
Gingerbread, 74
Glazed Fruit Salad, 78
Golden Potato Casserole, 118
Goodbye Turkey Casserole, 123
Good Luck Blackeyed Peas, 17
Gravy—Smooth 'N Easy, 164
Green Bean Casserole, 36
Green Chili Hominy, 147
Green Chili Souffle, 147
Green Vegetable Medley, 29
Grit Casserole, 109
Ground Beef Special, 139
Guacamole Dip, 59

H

Ham and Cheese Rolls, 131
Ham Dip, 5
Ham Loaf, 142

Hello Dollies, 77
Helpful Hints, 169-170
Herbed Chicken, 144
Holiday Cranberry Cake, 157
Homemade Chicken Broth, 165
Honey Cornmeal Biscuits, 36
Horseradish Roast, 23
Hot Cinnamon Apple Punch, 115
Hot Cranberry Punch, 82
Hot Dogs in Sweet and Sour Sauce, 91
Hot Mulled Pineapple, 98
Hot Orange Cider, 72
Hot Punch, 93
Hot Spiced Punch, 4

I

Ice Cream Sundae Dessert, 47

J

Jalapeno Grits Casserole, 41
Jam—Peach and Raspberry Jam, 163
Jello Punch, 65

K

Kahlua Crunch, 76
Key Lime Macadamia Dream Pie, 160
Key Lime Pie, 30
Knorr's Spinach Dip, 15

L

Lasagna, 141
Layered Broccoli Salad, 65
Lemon Herb Potatoes, 67
Lemon Sauce, 74
Lemonade with Frozen Tea Cubes, 130
Lipton California Dip, 5

M

Main Dishes
  Beef Stroganoff, 139
  Black Bean Soup, 136
  Brisket, 52
  Brunch Egg Casserole, 7
  Candied Ham Loaf with Mustard Sauce, 66
  Chicken and Dressing Casserole, 143
  Chicken in a Sack, 83
  Chicken Tetrazzini, 101
  Coffee Flavored Pot Roast, 145
  Cranberry Burgundy Glazed Ham, 35
  Do-Ahead Breakfast Souffle, 109
  Do-Ahead Sausage Souffle, 40
  Easy Day Stew, 136
  Goodbye Turkey Casserole, 123
  Ground Beef Special, 139
  Ham Loaf, 142
  Herbed Chicken, 144

Horseradish Roast, 23
Lasagna, 141
Meatloaf Supreme, 140
Nutty Baked Chicken, 143
Peanut Butter Soup, 137
Salmon Loaf, 138
Southern Shrimp and
  Chicken, 138
Spicy Chicken with
  Peanuts, 144
Split Pea Soup, 137
Stuffed Pork Chops, 29
Sukiyaki, 142
Talerine, 46
Texas Casserole, 61
Turkey in a Sack, 116
Veal Parmesan, 145
Wild Rice and Ham
  Chowder, 92
Yummy Baked Chicken with
  Rice, 16
Maple Pecan Pie, 119
Marinate—Steak Marinate, 164
Marinated Beans, 23
Meatloaf Supreme, 140
Melt-in-Your-Mouth
  Biscuits, 150
Mexican Salad, 60
Microwave Shortcuts, 175-178
Milky Way Cake, 73
Mini-Morsel Muffins, 73
Mint Julep, 129
Minted Fruit Bowl, 135
Mock Margarita, 58
Monkey Bread II, 54

N

90-Minute Pecan Corn-
  bread, 149
Nutty Baked Chicken, 143

O

Oatmeal Chocolate Chip
  Cookies, 94
Onion Cheese French Bread, 46
Open House Punch, 98
Orange Dressing for Fruit, 165
Orange Pecan Pie, 159
Orange Souffle Mold, 135
Oriental Hot Munch, 99

P

PTA Dessert, 54
Pancakes
  Ebelskievers, 152
  Sour Cream Pancakes, 151
  Swedish Pancakes, 152
Party Green Beans, 117
Peach and Raspberry Jam, 163
Peaches and Cream Cake, 157
Peaches or Pears Cardinale, 156
Peanut Brittle, 9
Peanut Butter Balls, 153
Peanut Butter Soup, 137
Pecan Cheese Ball, 100
Perfect Chocolate Cake, 17

Perfect Popovers, 150
Pies
  Brandy Cream Pie, 75
  Cherry Cream Cheese Pie, 86
  Date Nut Pie, 76
  Easy Millionaire Pie, 75
  French Silk Pie, 161
  French Strawberry Pie, 159
  Kahlua Crunch, 76
  Key Lime Macadamia Dream Pie, 160
  Key Lime Pie, 30
  Maple Pecan Pie, 119
  Orange Pecan Pie, 159
  Pumpkin Chiffon Pie, 87
  Strawberry Pie, 160
Pina Colada Cake, 10
Pineapple Casserole, 40
Pineapple Upside Down Cake, 73
Pink Salad, 34
Poppy Seed Cake, 111
Poppy Seed Cream Filling, 111
Pork
  Candied Ham Loaf, 66
  Cranberry Burgundy Glazed Ham, 35
  Do-Ahead Sausage Souffle, 40
  Ham Loaf, 142
  Sausage Pinwheels, 109
  Stuffed Pork Chops, 29
Potatoes
  Company Potatoes, 24
  Golden Potato Casserole, 118
  Lemon Herb Potatoes, 67
  Potato Casserole, 30
  Texas Potatoes, 84
Potpourri
  Cooking a Turkey, 173-174

  Gift Ideas, 171-172
  Helpful Hints, 169-170
  Microwave Shortcuts, 175-178
Pound Candy, 9
Praline Sauce, 163
Prune Cake, 102
Pumpkin Cake, 72
Pumpkin Chiffon Pie, 87
Punch with a "Punch," 51

R

Ranger Cookies, 153
Ribbon Salad, 83
Rice and Broccoli Casserole, 53
Ritz Bits Treats, 167
Russian Tea Mix, 167

S

St. Patrick's Punch, 28
Salad Dressings
  Orange Dressing for Fruit, 165
  Sunflower Salad Dressing, 166
  Whipped Cream Waldorf Salad Dressing, 166
Salads
  <u>Congealed</u>
    Cherry Jello Waldorf Salad, 28
    Orange Souffle Mold, 135
    Ribbon Salad, 83
  <u>Fruit</u>
    Bing Cherry Salad, 134
    Cherry Salad, 78
    Classic Waldorf Salad, 132
    Cranberry Grape Salad, 100
    Cranberry Relish

Oldtime, 115
Fresh Fruit Shell Salad, 132
Fruit with Poppy Seed
  Dressing, 7
Glazed Fruit Salad, 78
Minted Fruit Bowl, 135
Pink Salad, 34
Snowball Salad, 123
Sunburst Fruit Salad, 22
Watergate Salad, 133
Lettuce
  Crunchy Salad, 115
  Garden Salad with Almonds
    and Oranges, 16
  Mexican Salad, 60
  Tangerine Garden Salad, 108
  24-Hour Salad, 82
  Wilted Lettuce, 134
Meat
  Chicken Fruit Salad, 133
Slaw
  Backyard Coleslaw, 52
  Carrot Slaw, 100
Vegetable
  Cauliflower Salad, 34
  Corn Marinate, 61
  Dijon Potato Salad, 132
  English Pea Salad, 91
  Layered Broccoli Salad, 65
  Marinated Beans, 23
  Spinach Cottage Cheese
    Salad, 45
Salmon Loaf, 138
Salmon Party Roll, 131
Salsa Pronto, 165
Sangria Punch, 58
Sauces
  Dessert
    Caramel Pecan Sauce, 164
    Lemon Sauce, 74
    Praline Sauce, 163
    Toffee Fudge Sauce, 163
  Fluffy Mustard Sauce, 66
  Salsa Pronto, 165
Sausage Pinwheels, 109
Scrumptious Jam Cake with
  Filling, 110
Smooth 'n Easy Gravy, 164
Smoothie, 40
Snappy Carrots, 53
Snowball Salad, 123
Snowman Cake, 120
Soup
  Black Bean Soup, 136
  Clear Tomato Soup, 22
  Homemade Chicken Broth, 165
  Peanut Butter Soup, 137
  Split Pea Soup, 137
  Tortilla Soup, 60
  Wild Rice and Ham
    Chowder, 92
Sour Cream Pancakes, 151
Southern Shrimp and
  Chicken, 138
Spiced Orange Ginger Tea, 91
Spicy Chicken with Peanuts, 144
Spinach Cottage Cheese
  Salad, 45
Spinach Souffle Baked in
  Squash, 148
Split Pea Soup, 137
Steak Marinade, 164
Strawberry Bread, 41
Strawberry Cake, 25
Strawberry Candy, 25
Strawberry Crush, 129
Strawberry Pie, 160
Stuffed Pork Chops, 29
Stuffing—Apple, Apricot, Currant, and Pecan Stuffing, 84

Sukiyaki, 142
Sunburst Fruit Salad, 22
Sunflower Salad Dressing, 166
Swedish Pancakes, 152
Sweet Potato Casserole, 35
Sweet Potato Casserole in Orange Cups, 85
Sweet Potatoes with Marshmallows, 118
Sweet Roll Biscuits, 8

T

Talerine, 46
Tangerine Garden Salad, 108
Tasty Vegetable Dip, 5
Texas Casserole, 61
Texas Potatoes, 84
Tex-Mex Dip, 51
Toffee Fudge Sauce, 163
Toll House Cookie Brittle, 153
Tortilla Soup, 60
Tupperware Bread, 68
Turkey
  Cooking a Turkey, 173-174
  Goodbye Turkey Casserole, 123
  Turkey in a Sack, 116
24-Hour Salad, 82

V

Veal Parmesan, 145
Vegetables
  Baked Acorn Squash, 147
  Baked Beans, 67
  Blackeyed Pea Stew, 148
  Broccoli Balls, 101
  Broccoli Carrot Casserole, 117
  Buttered Carrots and Celery, 24
  Celery Amandine, 146
  Company Potatoes, 24
  Corn Marinate, 61
  French Bean Casserole, 85
  Good Luck Blackeyed Peas, 17
  Green Bean Casserole, 36
  Green Chili Hominy, 147
  Green Chili Souffle, 147
  Green Vegetable Medley, 29
  Golden Potato Casserole, 118
  Lemon Herb Potatoes, 67
  Marinated Beans, 23
  Party Green Beans, 117
  Potato Casserole, 30
  Rice and Broccoli Casserole, 53
  Snappy Carrots, 53
  Spinach Souffle Baked in Squash, 148

Sweet Potato Casserole, 35
Sweet Potato Casserole in
   Orange Cups, 85
Sweet Potatoes with
   Marshmallows, 118
Texas Potatoes, 84
Yellow Squash, 146

W

Watergate Salad, 133
Whipped Cream Pralines, 62
Whipped Cream Waldorf Salad
   Dressing, 166
White Grape Juice Spritzer, 72
Wild Rice and Ham Chowder, 92
Wilted Lettuce, 134
Winter Cocoa Mix, 167
Winter Fruit Splendor, 154
Winter Spiced Pears and
   Apples, 108

Y

Yellow Squash, 146
Yummy Baked Chicken with
   Rice, 16